DEATH, AFTERLIFE,
AND ESCHATOLOGY

DEATH, AFTERLIFE, AND ESCHATOLOGY

A Thematic Source Book of the
History of Religions

Part 3 of *FROM PRIMITIVES TO ZEN*

MIRCEA ELIADE

1817

HARPER & ROW, PUBLISHERS
NEW YORK, EVANSTON, SAN FRANCISCO, LONDON

ISBN: 0-06-062139-7

LIBRARY OF CONGRESS CATALOG CARD NUMBER: 73-20493

First Harper & Row paperback published 1974. This book contains chapter IV of FROM PRIMITIVES TO ZEN.

Preface to the Paperback Edition

The instigation for this anthology of religious texts and its three companion volumes came during my first years of teaching History of Religions at the University of Chicago. In discussing a specific problem, I expected my students to read at least some of the basic original sources; but I soon discovered that I was unable to recommend to them any single work where one might find a number of essential texts regarding, for example, high gods, cosmogonic myths, conceptions of death and the afterlife, etc. Although we have many source books, some of them excellent, for the most important religions, there were then no comprehensive anthologies in English presenting religious documents according to themes and topics. It seems to me that only by reading a certain number of religious texts related to the same subject (cosmogony, initiation, myths on the origin of death, etc.) is a student able to grasp their structural similarities and their differences.

Any thematic classification of religious documents implies a certain amount of arbitrariness. Some of the texts located under one classification could just as well have been integrated into another classification. But this source book is designed to be *read* first, from beginning to end, and only afterward to be *consulted*. A cross-reference index will help the reader, if he so wishes, to examine consecutively all the documents related to a specific religion or a particular cultural-geographic area such as Mesopotamia, Ancient Greece, India (or again just one segment of Indian religion: Vedism, Brahmanism, Buddhism, etc.), or the 'primitives' (but also just Australia, Oceania, Africa, Asia, North or South America).

A disturbing problem was raised by the respective proportions to be allotted to the documents representing the different religions and cultural-geographic areas. I was understandably eager to include the most representative religious texts; on the other hand, the thematic classification compelled me to illustrate all the important religious beliefs, conceptions, rituals, and institutions. Thus, for example, because I selected copiously from the *Tao Tê Ching,* the Vedic hymns, and the *Upanishads,* I was compelled to be sparing with Chinese and Indian rituals.

For obvious reasons, only a limited number of documents could be reprinted *in toto.* Omissions in the body of the text are indicated by ellipsis points. In the case of long documents, portions omitted are summarized. In rare cases, when the text was unusually long, I gave a résumé with long quotations. Explanatory notes are restricted to bare essentials; in many instances, I made use of or adapted the translator's notes. When it seemed necessary, I introduced a document or a group of documents with a brief comment. My own comments are printed in italics. Commentaries by others are printed in the same type as the documents they accompany; credit is given in the source line for the document. The use of parentheses and brackets within the documents reprinted follows the style of the book from which the particular selection was taken.

I have tried to avoid using materials from books and periodicals that are rare or hard to get. Thus the reader interested in a specific topic can find additional documents in rather easily accessible publications. The selective bibliography at the end of the volume was prepared with the same end in view: only the most useful and important books are listed. Whenever I could cite a monograph on a specific subject containing a rich and well-organized bibliography, I thought it unnecessary to quote other works.

I have made use only of existing English translations of sacred texts. In the case of Ancient Near Eastern, Indian, Greek, Chinese, and Japanese texts, I chose from all the competent translations available, in order to convey to the reader the various possibilities for rendering such abstruse and nonfamiliar texts. In selecting documents related to the 'primitive,' pre-literate societies, I followed the same principle: I limited my choice to works written in, or translated into, English. I hasten to add that although the term 'primitive' is misleading, and should be replaced by 'pre-literate' or 'archaic,' I have kept it, with the majority of authors, for reasons of convenience.

I have tried to include documents from almost all the important religious traditions, from primitive religion to the Ancient Near East to Islam, late Buddhism, and Zen. I have not included Hittite and Ugaritic texts, however, because their fragmentary condition would have demanded too extensive a commentary; furthermore, there are many readily available and competent translations of such texts. A more serious omission is that of Judaism and Christianity. But one cannot present these religions without quoting extensively from the Old and New Testaments, and it seemed unwise to increase the bulk and price of this source book considerably by reproducing such well-known texts. However, companion volumes presenting the Judaic and Christian documents on a somewhat similar thematic basis would be timely. For the moment, the omission of Judaism and Christianity may give the reader a rather inexact idea of the novelty and uniqueness of Muhammad's prophetic experience and of Islamic mystical and theological speculations on the One God. But of course I am assuming that the majority of readers will know something of the other two older monotheistic traditions.

No author of such anthology can hope to satisfy all of his colleagues or, even less so, all of his readers. No matter how 'objective' an author may be in collecting, classifying, and presenting religious documents, his choice is ultimately a personal one. But I should like to point out that this book must be judged as a whole, and not from the particular viewpoint of the anthropologist, or the classical scholar, or the orientalist. As I have already said, the book was conceived as one to be read from beginning to end, and not merely consulted. For the same reason I have tried to limit the scientific apparatus to a minimum. I have not intended to bring out another scholarly work for the exclusive use of the scholar, but a simple and readable book accessible to any *honnête homme* curious about the religious beliefs of his fellow men.

I have to thank my friend and colleague Professor Joseph Kitagawa for helping me in the selection of Japanese materials, Mrs. Rehova Arthur for carefully typing a great portion of the manuscript, Mr. Alan Miller for reading a number of Islamic texts, and Mr. David Knipe for editing and providing notes (not otherwise credited) to the Indian and Scandinavian materials. I am grateful to Miss Nancy Auer for typing and editing most of the Mesopotamian documents, for helping me at various stages of the work, and also for reading and correcting the proofs. Finally, I am thankful to my wife not only for typing a certain number of texts, but especially for encouraging me to continue and complete this work, which kept me intermittently busy for five years. Of course, had I known that so much work would be involved, I would not have dared to embark on such a project. My one consolation for the time and energy consumed is that this source book and its three companion volumes will help the student and the interested reader to confront and understand the religious life of ancient and non-Western man.

MIRCEA ELIADE

University of Chicago

Publisher's Note to the Paperback Edition

The selections in *From Primitives to Zen* are numbered consecutively from no. 1 to no. 306. The consecutive numbering is retained in this paperback edition to facilitate the use of the cross-reference system. Nos. 1-74 are contained in *Gods, Goddesses, and Myths of Creation;* nos. 75-157 in *Man and the Sacred;* nos. 158-197 in *Death, Afterlife, and Eschatology;* nos. 198-306 in *From Medicine Men to Muhammad.*

Contents

DEATH, AFTERLIFE, ESCHATOLOGY

Contents

Contents

Death, Afterlife, and Eschatology

A. GODS, HEROES, AND DEATH

158. THE DESCENT OF ISHTAR TO THE NETHER WORLD

Ishtar, goddess of life and fertility, decides to visit her sister Ereshkigal, goddess of death and sterility. As Ishtar forces her way through the gates of the nether world, her robes and garments are stripped from her. Naked and helpless, she finally reaches Ereshkigal, who instantly has her put to death. Without Ishtar, there is no fertility on earth, and the gods soon realize their loss. Ea creates the beautiful eunuch Asushunamir, who tricks Ereshkigal into reviving Ishtar with the water of life and releasing her. The ending of the myth is obscure; perhaps Ishtar's lover, Tammuz, was released along with her. Like the Gilgamesh Epic the myth of the descent of Ishtar to the nether world has its Sumerian counterpart (see S. N. Kramer, 'Inanna's Descent to the Nether World,' ANET, pp. 52-7). Yet the Akkadian version differs substantially from its Sumerian prototype and is by no means a slavish translation of the former. The Sumerian version of the myth dates from the first half of the second millennium B.C.; the Semitic versions do not antedate the end of the second millennium B.C.

To the Land of no Return, the realm of Ereshkigal,
Ishtar, the daughter of Sin, set her mind.
Yea, the daughter of Sin set her mind
To the dark house, the abode of Irkalla,[1]
To the house which none leave who have entered it,
To the road from which there is no way back,
To the house wherein the dwellers are bereft of light,
Where dust is their fare and clay their food,
(Where) they see no light, residing in darkness,
(Where) they are clothed like birds, with wings for garments,
(And where) over door and bolt is spread dust.
When Ishtar reached the gate of the Land of no Return,

She said (these) words to the gatekeeper:
'O gatekeeper, open thy gate,
Open thy gate that I may enter!
If thou openest not the gate so that I cannot enter,
I will smash the door, I will shatter the bolt,
I will smash the doorpost, I will move the doors,
I will raise up the dead, eating the living,
So that the dead will outnumber the living.'
The gatekeeper opened his mouth to speak,
Saying to exalted Ishtar:
'Stop, my lady, do not throw it[2] down!
I will go to announce they name to Queen Ereshkigal.'
The gatekeeper entered, saying to Ereshkigal:
'Behold, thy sister Ishtar is waiting at the gate,
She who upholds the great festivals,
   Who stirs up the deep before Ea, the king.'
When Ereshkigal heard this,
Her face turned pale like a cut-down tamarisk,
While her lips turned dark like a bruised kunīnu-reed.
'What drove her heart to me? What impelled her spirit hither?
Lo, should I drink water with the Anunnaki?
Should I eat clay for bread, drink muddied water for beer?
Should I bemoan the men who left their wives behind?
Should I bemoan the maidens who were wrenched from the laps of
   their lovers?
(Or) should I bemoan the tender little one who was sent off before his
   time?[3]
Go, gatekeeper, open the gate for her,
Treat her in accordance with the ancient rules.'
Forth went the gatekeeper (to) open the door for her:
'Enter, my lady, that Cutha[4] may rejoice over thee,
That the palace of the Land of no Return may be glad at thy presence.'
When the first door he had made her enter,
   He stripped and took away the great crown on her head.
'Why O gatekeeper, didst thou take the great crown on my head?'
'Enter, my lady, thus are the rules of the Mistress of the Nether World.'

[*Ishtar passes through seven gates of the nether world. At each of
them the gatekeeper removes an ornament. At the second gate, he takes
the pendants on her ears; at the third, the chains round her neck; then
he removes, respectively, the ornaments on her breast, the girdle of*

birthstones on her hips, the clasps round her hands and feet, and the breechcloth on her body. Each time, she asks the same question; each time she receives the same answer.]

As soon as Ishtar had descended to the Land of no Return,
Ereshkigal saw her and was enraged at her presence.
Ishtar, unreasoning, flew at her.
Ereshkigal opened her mouth to speak,
Saying (these) words to Namtar, her vizier:
'Go, Namtar, lock her up in my palace!
Release against her, against Ishtar, the sixty miseries:
Misery of the eyes against her eyes,
Misery of the sides against her sides,
Misery of the feet against her feet,
Misery of the head against her head—
Against every part of her, against her whole body!'
After Lady Ishtar had descended to the Land of no Return,
The bull springs not upon the cow, the ass impregnates not the jenny,
In the street the man impregnates not the maiden.
The man lay in his (own) chamber, the maiden lay on her side.
....
The countenance of Papsukkal, the vizier of the great gods,
    Was fallen, his face was clouded.
He was clad in mourning, long hair he wore.
Forth went Papsukkal before Sin his father, weeping,
His tears flowing before Ea, the king:
'Ishtar has gone down to the nether world, she has not come up.
Since Ishtar has gone down to the Land of no Return,
The bull springs not upon the cow, the ass impregnates not the jenny,
In the street the man impregnates not the maiden.
The man lay down in his (own) chamber,
The maiden lay down on her side.'
Ea in his wise heart conceived an image,
And created Asushunamir, a eunuch:
'Up, Asushunamir, set thy face to the gate of the Land of no Return;
The seven gates of the Land of no Return shall be opened for thee.
Ereshkigal shall see thee and rejoice at thy presence.
When her heart is calmed, her mood is happy,
Let her utter the oath of the great gods.
(Then) lift up thy head, paying mind to the life-water bag:
'Pray, Lady, let them give me the life-water bag

That water therefrom I may drink.'[5]
As soon as Ereshkigal heard this,
She smote her thigh, bit her finger:
'Thou didst request of me a thing that should not be requested.
Come, Asushunamir, I will curse thee with a mighty curse!
The food of the city's plows[6] shall be thy food,
The sewers of the city shall be thy drink.
The shadow of the wall shall be thy station,
The threshold shall be thy habitation,
The besotted and the thirsty shall smite thy cheek!'
Ereshkigal opened her mouth to speak,
Saying (these) words to Namtar, her vizier:
'Ea, Namtar, knock at Egalgina,[7]
Adorn the thresholds with coral-stone,
Bring forth the Annunaki and seat (them) on thrones of gold,
Sprinkle Ishtar with the water of life and take her from my presence!'
Forth went Namtar, knocked at Egalgina.
Adorned the thresholds with coral-stone,
Brought forth the Anunnaki, seated (them) on thrones of gold,
Sprinkled Ishtar with the water of life and took her from her presence.
When through the first gate he had made her go out,
　　He returned to her the breechcloth for her body.

[As Ishtar passes through each of the seven gates, her ornaments are
returned to her one by one.]

'If she does not give thee her ransom price, bring her back.[8]
As for Tammuz, the lover of her youth,
Wash him with pure water, anoint him with sweet oil;
Clothe him with a red garment, let him play on a flute of lapis.
Let courtesans turn his mood.'
When Belili[9] had . . . her jewelry,
And her lap was filled with 'eye-stones,'[10]
On hearing the sound of her brother, Belili struck the jewelry on . . .
So that the 'eye-stones' filled her chamber.
'My only brother, bring no harm to me!
On the day when Tammuz welcomes me,
　　When with him the lapis flute (and) the carnelian ring welcome me,
When with him the wailing men and the wailing women welcome me,
May the dead rise and smell the incense.'

Notes

1 Another name of Ereshkigal, the queen of the nether world.
2 The door.
3 I.e. Ereshkigal would have cause for weeping if all these occupants of the nether world should be liberated by Ishtar.
4 A name of the nether world.
5 The scheme evidently succeeds, as Ereshkigal, distracted by the beauty of Asushunamir (meaning 'His Appearance is brilliant'), does not recover until it is too late.
6 This probably means 'dirt.'
7 'Palace of Justice.'
8 The concluding part of the myth and its allusions, particularly to Tammuz are obscure.
9 Apparently referring to Ishtar.
10 'Beads'?

> Translation by E. A. Speiser, *Ancient Near Eastern Texts* (Princeton, 1950), pp. 106-9; reprinted in Isaac Mendelsohn (ed.), *Religions of the Ancient Near East*, Library of Religion paperbook series (New York, 1955), pp. 119-25; notes by Mendelsohn

159. GILGAMESH IN SEARCH OF IMMORTALITY

Although originally written in Akkadian, the Gilgamesh Epic was translated into several Near Eastern languages and became the most famous literary creation of the ancient Babylonians. Gilgamesh, king of Uruk, is two-thirds god and one-third man, and 'like a wild ox.' As the story begins, the nobles of Uruk are complaining to the gods that the mighty Gilgamesh in his restlessness and arrrogance is playing havoc with the city. His mother, the goddess Aruru, creates a companion for him—the wild man Enkidu, who runs with the animals on the steppe. Enkidu is first tamed and made human by a temple harlot. Then he is taken to Uruk, where he wrestles with Gilgamesh. The match is a draw and the two become inseparable companions.

One day, Gilgamesh, always looking for adventure, proposes that he and Enkidu travel to the distant cedar forest to kill Huwawa, its evil guardian. Enkidu protests that the journey is very dangerous and Huwawa very fierce, but Gilgamesh is determined and finally they set out. The undertaking is successful and the two are covered with glory.

But Enkidu has already had premonitions of disaster. On their return to Uruk, the goddess Ishtar sees the beauty of Gilgamesh and proposes to him. He rejects her, reminding her of the fates of her previous lovers. She is furious and has Anu send the sacred bull of heaven to attack him. When Gilgamesh and Enkidu slay the bull, the gods become very angry—this is too presumptuous. As punishment, Enkidu must die.

Enkidu's death is the occasion for the section which we have included here, the climax and culmination of the Epic. For the first time Gilgamesh has had to face the fact of death, and it bewilders and terrifies him. Hoping to learn the secret of immortality, he makes a long and difficult journey in search of Utnapishtim, the one human being who has acquired it. Utnapishtim tells his story—the famous story of the flood. But Gilgamesh is, after all, human and very tired. He falls asleep. Utnapishtim is about to send him away when his wife intervenes in pity. Gilgamesh is told about a wonderful plant of immortality that grows at the bottom of the sea. He obtains it; but as he stops to cool himself in a quiet pool a snake carries off the plant. Gilgamesh, completely unsuccessful, returns to Uruk, and the text concludes as he proudly shows his city to his ferryman.

For Enkidu, his friend, Gilgamesh
Weeps bitterly, as he ranges over the steppe:
'When I die, shall I not be like Enkidu?
Woe has entered my belly.
Facing death, I roam over the steppe.
To Utnapishtim,[1] Ubar-Tutu's son,
I have taken the road to proceed in all haste.
When arriving by night at mountain passes,
I saw lions and grew afraid.
I lifted my head to Sin[2] to pray.

[The remainder of the column is fragmentary or broken away. When Gilgamesh next appears, he has arrived before a mountain.]

The name of the mountain is Mashu.
When he arrived at the mountain range of Mashu,
Which daily keeps watch over sunrise and sunset—
Whose peaks reach to the vault of heaven
(And) whose breasts reach to the nether world below—
Scorpion-men guard its gate,
Whose terror is awesome and whose glance was death.
Their shimmering halo sweeps the mountains
That at sunrise and sunset keep watch over the sun.

Gods, Heroes, and Death

When Gilgamesh beheld them, with fear
And terror was darkened his face.
He took hold of his senses and bowed before them.
A scorpion-man calls to his wife:
'He who has come to us—his body is the flesh of the gods!'
His wife answers the scorpion-man:
'Two-thirds of him is god, one-third of him is human.'
The scorpion-man calls to the fellow,
Addressing (these) words to the offspring of the gods:
'Why hast thou come on this far journey?
Why hast thou arrived before me,
Traversing seas whose crossings are difficult?
The purpose of thy coming I would learn.'

[The remainder of the column is broken away. In the next part that
we have, Gilgamesh replies:]

'On account of Utnapishtim, my father, have I come,
Who joined the Assembly of the gods, in search of life.
About death and life I wish to ask him.'
The scorpion-man opened his mouth to speak,
Saying to Gilgamesh:
'Never was there, Gilgamesh, a mortal who could achieve that.
The mountain's trail no one has travelled.
For twelve leagues extends its inside.
Dense is the darkness and light there is none.

[The remainder is fragmentary or broken. Gilgamesh persists, and
eventually the scorpion-man opens the mountain to him.]

When Gilgamesh heard this,
To the word of the scorpion-man he gave heed.
Along the road of the sun he went.[3]
When one league he had attained,
Dense is the darkness and light there is none;
He can see nothing ahead or behind.

[Gilgamesh travels for eight leagues in total blackness. Beginning the
the ninth league, he feels the north wind fanning his face. He gradually
emerges from the cave.]

When eleven leagues he had attained, the dawn breaks.
And when he had attained twelve leagues, it had grown bright.
On seeing the grove of stones, he heads for . . .

The carnelian bears its fruit;
It is hung with vines good to look at.
The lapis bears foliage;
It, too, bears fruit lush to behold.

[*The remainder of the tablet is mutilated or lost. There are two fairly complete versions of the episodes in the following tablet—the Old Babylonian and Assyrian recensions—as well as two, more fragmentary, versions. We shall begin with the Old Babylonian version. The top of the tablet is broken.*]

Shamash was distraught, as he betook himself to him;
He says to Gilgamesh:
'Gilgamesh, whither rovest thou?
The life thou pursuest thou shalt not find.'
Gilgamesh says to him, to valiant Shamash:
'After marching (and) roving over the steppe,
Must I lay my head in the heart of the earth
That I may sleep through all the years?
Let mine eyes behold the sun
   That I may have my fill of the light!
Darkness withdraws when there is enough light.
May he who has died a death behold the radiance of the sun!'

[*Again there is a break in the text. Gilgamesh is addressing Siduri,*[4] *the ale-wife, who, according to the Assyrian text, 'dwells by the deep sea.'*]

'He who with me underwent all hardships—
Enkidu, whom I loved dearly,
Who with me underwent all hardships—
Has now gone to the fate of mankind!
Day and night I have wept over him.
I would not give him up for burial—
In case my friend should rise at my plaint—
Seven days and seven nights,
Until a worm fell out of his nose.
Since his passing I have not found life,
I have roamed like a hunter in the midst of the steppe.
O ale-wife, now that I have seen thy face,
Let me not see the death which I ever dread.'
The ale-wife said to him, to Gilgamesh:
'Gilgamesh, whither rovest thou?

The life thou pursuest thou shalt not find.
When the gods created mankind,
Death for mankind they set aside,
Life in their own hands retaining.
Thou, Gilgamesh, let full be thy belly,
Make thou merry by day and by night.
Of each day make thou a feast of rejoicing,
Day and night dance thou and play!
Let thy garments be sparkling fresh,
Thy head be washed; bathe thou in water.
Pay heed to the little one that holds on to thy hand,
Let thy spouse delight in thy bosom!
For this is the task of mankind!'

[The remainder of the conversation is lost. The Assyrian text gives a different version of Siduri's response.]

Gilgamesh also says to her, to the ale-wife:
'Now ale-wife, which is the way to Utnapishtim?
What are its markers? Give me, O give me, its markers!
If it be possible, the sea I will cross;
If it not be possible, over the steppe I will range!'
The ale-wife said to him, to Gilgamesh:
'Never, O Gilgamesh, has there been a crossing,
And none who came since the beginning of days could cross the sea.
Only valiant Shamash crosses the sea;
    Other than Shamash who can cross (it)?
Toilsome is the place of crossing
    Very toilsome the way thereto,
And deep are the Waters of Death that bar its approaches!
Where then, O Gilgamesh, wouldst thou cross the sea?
On reaching the Waters of Death, what wouldst thou do?
Gilgamesh, there is Urshanabi, boatman to Utnapishtim.
With him are the Stone Things.[5] In the woods he picks 'urnu'-snakes.[6]
Him let thy face behold.
If it be suitable, cross thou with him.
    If it be not suitable, draw thou back.'
When Gilgamesh heard this,
He raised the axe in his hand,
Drew the dirk from his belt, slipped into (the forest),
    And went down to them.[7]
Like an arrow he descended among them.

[*The text is too fragmentary for translation. When it resumes, Gilgamesh is responding to Urshanabi's questions. He again tells of Enkidu's death and his own search and asks how he can find Utnapishtim. Urshanabi warns him that, by breaking the 'Stone Things,' he has hindered his own crossing. But he agrees to guide Gilgamesh, and sends him off to cut poles. They set sail and soon come to the waters of death, where Urshanabi instructs Gilgamesh: 'Press on, Gilgamesh, take a pole, / (But) let thy hand not touch the Waters of Death . . . !' Finally they reach Utnapishtim's island. Utnapishtim questions Gilgamesh, who repeats his long story again, concluding it as follows.*]

Gilgamesh also said to him, to Utnapishtim:
'That now I might come and behold Utnapishtim,
   Whom they call the Faraway,
I ranged and wandered over all the lands,
I traversed difficult mountains,
I crossed all the seas!
My face was not sated with sweet sleep,
I fretted myself with wakefulness;
I filled my joints with aches.
I had not reached the ale-wife's house
   When my clothing was used up.
I slew bear, hyena, lion, panther,
   Tiger, stag, (and) ibex—
The wild beasts and the creeping things of the steppe.
Their flesh I ate and their skins I wrapped about me.'

[*The remainder of the tablet is fragmentary and broken, except for the conclusion to Utnapishtim's response.*]

'Do we build houses for ever?
   Do we seal (contracts) for ever?
Do brothers divide shares for ever?
Does hatred persist for ever in the land?
Does the river for ever rise (and) bring on floods?
The dragon-fly leave (its) shell
That its face might (but) glance on the face of the sun?
Since the days of yore there has been no performance;
The resting and the dead, how alike they are!
Do they not compose a picture of death,
The commoner and the noble,
   Once they are near to their fate?
The Anunnaki, the great gods, foregather;

Mammetum, *maker of fate, with them the fate decrees;*
Death and life they determine.
(But) of death its days are not revealed.'
Gilgamesh said to him, to Utnapishtim the Faraway:
'As I look upon thee, Utnapishtim,
Thy features are not strange; even as I art thou.
My heart had regarded thee as resolved to do battle,
Yet thou liest indolent upon my back!
Tell me, how joinedst thou the Assembly of the gods,
    In thy quest of life?'
Utnapishtim said to him, to Gilgamesh:
'I will reveal to thee, Gilgamesh, a hidden matter
And a secret of the gods will I tell thee: . . .'

[Utnapishtim's revelation is the flood narrative. He was made immortal, he says, through the intervention of the gods after he managed to survive the great flood which destroyed Shurippak.]

'But now, who will for thy sake call the gods to Assembly
That the life which thou seekest thou mayest find?
Up, lie down to sleep
    For six days and seven nights.'
As he sits there on his haunches,
Sleep fans him like a mist.
Utnapishtim says to her, to his spouse:
'Behold this hero who seeks life!
Sleep fans him like a mist.'
His spouse says to him, to Utnapishtim the Faraway:
'Touch him that the man may awake,
That he may return safe on the way back whence he came,
That through the gate he left he may return to his land.'
Utnapishtim says to her, to his spouse:
'Since to deceive is human, he will seek to deceive thee.[8]
Up, bake for him wafers, put (them) at his head,
And mark on the walls the days he sleeps.'
She baked for him wafers, put (them) at his head,
And marked on the wall the days he slept.
His first wafer is dried out,
The second is leathery, the third is soggy;
    The crust of the fourth has turned white;
The fifth has a mouldy cast,
    The sixth (still) is fresh coloured;

And just as he touched the seventh, the man awoke.
Gilgamesh says to him, to Utnapishtim the Faraway:
'Scarcely had sleep surged over me,
When straightway thou dost touch and rouse me!'
Utnapishtim says to him, to Gilgamesh:
'Go, Gilgamesh, count thy wafers,
That the days thou hast slept may become known to thee:
Thy first wafer is dried out
The second is leathery, the third is soggy;
   The crust of the fourth has turned white;
The fifth has a mouldy cast,
   The sixth (still) is fresh coloured.
As for the seventh, at this instant thou hast awakened.'
Gilgamesh says to him, to Utnapishtim the Faraway:
'What then shall I do, Utnapishtim,
   Whither shall I go,
Now that the Bereaver has laid hold on my members?
In my bedchamber lurks death,
And wherever I set my foot, there is death!'
Utnapishtim says to him, to Urshanabi, the boatman:
'Urshanabi, may the landing-place not rejoice in thee,
   May the place of the crossing despise thee!
To him who wanders on its shore, deny thou its shore!
The man thou hast led (hither), whose body is covered with grime,
The grace of whose members skins have distorted,
Take him, Urshanabi, and bring him to the washing-place.
Let him wash off his grime in water clean as snow,
Let him cast off his skins, let the sea carry (them) away,
   That the fairness of his body may be seen.
Let him renew the band round his head,
Let him put on a cloak to clothe his nakedness,
That he may arrive in his city,
That he may achieve his journey.
Let not (his) cloak have a mouldy cast,
   Let it be wholly new.'
Urshanabi took him and brought him to the washing-place.
He washed off his grime in water clean as snow.
He cast off his skins, the sea carried (them) away,
That the fairness of his body might be seen.
He renewed the band round his head,
He put on a cloak to clothe his nakedness,

That he might arrive in his city,
That he might achieve his journey.
The cloak had not a mouldy cast, but was wholly new.
Gilgamesh and Urshanabi boarded the boat,
They launched the boat on the waves (and) they sailed away.
His spouse says to him, to Utnapishtim the Faraway:
'Gilgamesh has come hither, toiling and straining.
What wilt thou give him that he may return to his land?'
At that he, Gilgamesh, raised up (his) pole,
To bring the boat nigh to the shore.
Utnapishtim says to him, to Gilgamesh:
'Gilgamesh, thou hast come hither, toiling and straining.
What shall I give thee that thou mayest return to thy land?
I will disclose, O Gilgamesh, a hidden thing,
And . . . about a plant I will tell thee:
This plant, like the buckthorn is its . . .
Its thorns will prick thy hands just as does the rose.
If thy hands obtain the plant, thou wilt attain life.'
No sooner had Gilgamesh heard this,
    Than he opened the water-pipe,
He tied heavy stones to his feet.
They pulled him down into the deep and there he saw the plant.
He took the plant, though it pricked his hands.
He cut the heavy stones from his feet.
The sea cast him up upon its shore.
Gilgamesh says to him, to Urshanabi, the boatman:
'Urshanabi, this plant is a plant apart,
Whereby a man may regain his life's breath.
I will take it to ramparted Uruk,
    Will cause . . . to eat the plant . . . !
Its name shall be "Man Becomes Young in Old Age."
I myself shall eat (it)
    And thus return to the state of my youth.'
After twenty leagues they broke off a morsel,
After thirty (further) leagues they prepared for the night.
Gilgamesh saw a well whose water was cool.
He went down into it to bathe in the water.
A serpent snuffed the fragrance of the plant;
It came up from the water and carried off the plant.
Going back it shed its slough.
Thereupon Gilgamesh sits down and weeps,

His tears running down over his face.
He took the hand of Urshanabi, the boatman:
'For whom, Urshanabi, have my hands toiled?
For whom is being spent the blood of my heart?
I have not obtained a boon for myself.
For the earth-lion[9] have I effected a boon!
And now the tide will bear (it) twenty leagues away!
When I opened the water-pipe and spilled the gear,
I found that which had been placed as a sign for me:
  I shall withdraw,
And leave the boat on the shore!'
  After twenty leagues they broke off a morsel,
After thirty (further) leagues they prepared for the night.
  When they arrived in ramparted Uruk,
Gilgamesh says to him, to Urshanabi, the boatman:
'Go up, Urshanabi, walk on the ramparts of Uruk.
Inspect the base terrace, examine its brickwork,
  If its brickwork is not of burnt brick,
And if the Seven Wise Ones laid not its foundation.
One "sar"[10] is city, one sar orchards,
  One sar margin land; (further) the precinct of the Temple of Ishtar.
Three sar and the precinct comprise Uruk.'

Notes

1 The Babylonian hero of the Flood; in Sumerian his name is Ziusudra.
2 The moon-god.
3 Apparently from east to west.
4 The divine barmaid.
5 Apparently stone figures of unusual properties.
6 Meaning not clear. Perhaps some magic symbols possessing properties on a par with those of the Stone Things.
7 To the Stone Things.
8 By asserting that he had not slept at all.
9 An allusion to the serpent?
10 One sar is about 8,000 gallons.

Translation by E. A. Speiser, in *Ancient Near Eastern Texts* (Princeton, 1950), pp. 72-99, reprinted in Isaac Mendelsohn (ed.), *Religions of the Ancient Near East*, Library of Religion paperbook series (New York, 1955). pp. 47-115; notes by Mendelsohn

See also no. 73

B. DEATH AND THE INTERMEDIATE STATE

160. THE MOMENT OF DEATH AS DESCRIBED BY THE UPANISHADS

When this self gets to weakness, gets to confusedness, as it were, then the breaths gather round him. He takes to himself those particles of light and descends into the heart. When the person in the eye turns away, then he becomes non-knowing of forms.

[When his body grows weak and he becomes apparently unconscious, the dying man gathers his senses about him, completely withdraws their powers and descends into the heart. *Radhakrishnan.*]

He is becoming one, he does not see, they say; he is becoming one, he does not smell, they say; he is becoming one, he does not taste, they say; he is becoming one, he does not speak, they say; he is becoming one, he does not hear, they say; he is becoming one, he does not think, they say; he is becoming one, he does not touch, they say; he is becoming one, he does not know, they say. The point of his heart becomes lighted up and by that light the self departs either through the eye or through the head or through other apertures of the body. And when he thus departs, life departs after him. And when life thus departs, all the vital breaths depart after him. He becomes one with intelligence. What has intelligence departs with him. His knowledge and his work take hold of him as also his past experience. (*Brihad-āranyaka Upanishad*, IV, 4, 1-2.)

Verily, when a person departs from this world, he goes to the air. It opens out there for him like the hole of a chariot wheel. Through that he goes upwards. He goes to the sun. It opens out there for him like the hole of a *lambara*. Through that he goes upwards. He reaches the moon. It opens out there for him like the hole of a drum. Through that he goes upwards. He goes to the world free from grief, free from snow. There he dwells eternal years. (*ibid.*, V, 11, 1.)

S. Radhakrishnan (editor and translator), *The Principal Upanishads* (New York: Harper & Row, 1953), pp. 269-70, 296

161. THE BUDDHIST CONCEPTION OF THE INTERMEDIATE STATE

('Saddharma-smrityupasthāna Sūtra,' from chapter XXXIV*)*

The Chinese translation of this material (from which the present English translation was made) dates from ca. A.D. 542.

When a human being dies and is going to be reincarnated as a human being . . . when the time of his death is approaching he sees these signs: he sees a great rocky mountain lowering above him like a shadow. He thinks to himself, 'The mountain might fall down on top of me,' and he makes a gesture with his hand as though to ward off this mountain. His brothers and kinsmen and neighbours see him do this; but to them it seems that he is simply pushing out his hand into space. Presently the mountain seems to be made of white cloth and he clambers up this cloth. Then it seems to be made of red cloth. Finally, as the time of his death approaches he sees a bright light, and being unaccustomed to it at the time of his death he is perplexed and confused. He sees all sorts of things such as are seen in dreams, because his mind is confused. He sees his (future) father and mother making love, and seeing them a thought crosses his mind, a perversity (*viparyāsa*) arises in him. If he is going to be reborn as a man he sees himself making love with his mother and being hindered by his father; or if he is going to be reborn as a woman, he sees himself making love with his father and being hindered by his mother. It is at that moment that the Intermediate Existence is destroyed and life and consciousness arise and causality begins once more to work. It is like the imprint made by a die; the die is then destroyed but the pattern has been imprinted.

Translation by Arthur Waley, in Conze *et al*, *Buddhist Texts through the Ages* (Oxford: Bruno Cassirer (Publishers) Ltd., 1954)

Death and the Intermediate State

162. THE TIBETAN BOOK OF THE DEAD: DEATH AND INTERMEDIATE STATES

Bardo Thödol, 'The Tibetan Book of the Dead,' is a guide for the dead and dying. The first part, called Chikhai Bardo, describes the moment of death. The second part, Chönyid Bardo, deals with the states which supervene immediately after death. The third part, Sidpa Bardo, concerns the onset of the birth instinct and of prenatal events.

When the expiration hath ceased, the vital-force will have sunk into the nerve-centre of Wisdom[1] and the Knower[2] will be experiencing the Clear Light of the natural condition.[3] Then the vital force, being thrown backwards and flying downwards through the right and left nerves,[4] the Intermediate State (Bardo) momentarily dawns.

The above [directions] should be applied before [the vital force hath] rushed into the left nerve [after first having traversed the navel nerve-centre].

The time [ordinarily necessary for this motion of the vital-force] is as long as the inspiration is still present, or about the time required for eating a meal.

Then the manner of application [of the instructions] is:

When the breathing is about to cease, it is best if the Transference hath been applied efficiently; if [the application] hath been inefficient, then [address the deceased] thus:

O nobly-born [so and so by name], the time hath now come for thee to seek the Path [in reality]. Thy breathing is about to cease. Thy guru hath set thee face to face before with the Clear Light; and now thou art about to experience in its Reality in the Bardo state, wherein all things are like the void and cloudless sky, and the naked, spotless intellect is like unto a transparent vacuum without circumference or centre. At this moment, know thou thyself; and abide in that state. I, too, at this time, am setting thee face to face.

Having read this, repeat it many times in the ear of the person dying, even before the expiration hath ceased, so as to impress it on the mind [of the dying one].

If the expiration is about to cease, turn the dying one over on the right side, which posture is called the 'Lying Posture of a Lion.' The throbbing of the arteries [on the right and left side of the throat] is to be pressed.

If the person dying be disposed to sleep, or if the sleeping state advances, that should be arrested, and the arteries pressed gently but firmly. Thereby the vital-force will not be able to return from the median-nerve and will be sure to pass out through the Brahmanic aperture.[5] Now the real setting-face-to-face is to be applied.

At this moment, the first [glimpsing] of the *Bardo* of the Clear Light of Reality, which is the Infallible Mind of the Dharma-Kāya, is experienced by all sentient beings.

After the expiration hath completely ceased, press the nerves of sleep firmly; and, a lama, or a person higher or more learned than thyself, impress in these words, thus:

Reverend Sir, now that thou art experiencing the Fundamental Clear Light, try to abide in that state which now thou art experiencing.

And also in the case of any other person the reader shall set him face-to-face thus:

O nobly-born [so-and-so], listen. Now thou art experiencing the Radiance of the Clear Light of Pure Reality. Recognize it. O nobly-born, thy present intellect, in real nature void, not formed into anything as regards characteristics or colour, naturally void, is the very Reality, the All-Good.

Thine own intellect, which is now voidness, yet not to be regarded as of the voidness of nothingness, but as being the intellect itself, unobstructed, shining, thrilling, and blissful, is the very consciousness, the All-good Buddha.

Thine own consciousness, not formed into anything, in reality void, and the intellect, shining and blissful,—these two,—are inseparable. The union of them is the Dharma-Kāya state of Perfect Enlightenment.[6]

Thine own consciousness, shining, void, and inseparable from the Great Body of Radiance, hath no birth, nor death, and is the Immutable Light—Buddha Amitābha.

Knowing this is sufficient. Recognizing the voidness of thine own intellect to be Buddhahood, and looking upon it as beng thine own consciousness, is to keep thyself in the [state of the] divine mind of the Buddha.

Repeat this distinctly and clearly three or [even] seven times. That will recall to the mind [of the dying one] the former [i.e. when living] setting-face-to-face by the *guru*. Secondly, it will cause the naked consciousness to be recognized as the Clear Light; and, thirdly, recognizing one's own self [thus], one becometh permanently united with the Dharma-Kāya and liberation will be certain.

[*If when dying, one is familiar with this state, the wheel of rebirth is stopped and liberation is instantaneously achieved. But such spiritual efficiency is so very rare that the normal mental condition of the dying person is unequal to the supreme feat of holding on to the state in which the Clear Light shines. There follows a progressive descent into lower and lower states of the Bardo existence, and finally rebirth. Immediately after the first state of Chikhai Bardo comes the second stage, when the consciousness-principle leaves the body and says to itself: 'Am I dead, or am I not dead?' without being able to determine.*]

But even though the Primary Clear Light be not recognized, the Clear Light of the second *Bardo* being recognized, Liberation will be attained. If not liberated even by that, then that called the third *Bardo* or the *Chönyid Bardo* dawneth.

In this third stage of the *Bardo*, the karmic illusions come to shine. It is very important that this Great setting-face-to-face of the *Chönyid Bardo* be read: it hath much power and can do much good.

About this time [the deceased] can see that the share of food is being set aside, that the body is being stripped of its garments, that the place of the sleeping-rug is being swept;[7] can hear all the weeping and wailing of his friends and relatives, and, although he can see them and can hear them calling upon him, they cannot hear him calling upon them, so he goeth away displeased.

At that time, sounds, lights, and rays—all three—are experienced. These awe, frighten, and terrify, and cause much fatigue. At this moment, this setting-face-to-face with the *Bardo* [during the experiencing] of Reality is to be applied. Call the deceased by name, and correctly and distinctly explain to him, as follows:

O nobly-born, listen with full attention, without being distracted: There are six states of *Bardo*, namely: the natural state of *Bardo* while in the womb; the *Bardo* of the dream-state; the *Bardo* of ecstatic equilibrium, while in deep meditation; the *Bardo* of the moment of death; the *Bardo* [during the experiencing] of Reality; the *Bardo* of the inverse process of samsāric existence. These are the six.

O nobly-born, thou wilt experience three *Bardos*, the *Bardo* of the moment of death, the *Bardo* [during the experiencing] of Reality, and the *Bardo* while seeking rebirth. Of these three, up to yesterday, thou hadst experienced the *Bardo* of the moment of death. Although the Clear Light of Reality dawned upon thee, thou wert unable to hold on, and so thou hast to wander here. Now henceforth thou art going to experience the [other] two, the *Chönyid Bardo* and the *Sidpa Bardo*.[8]

Thou wilt pay undistracted attention to that with which I am about to set thee face to face, and hold on;

O nobly-born, that which is called death hath now come. Thou art departing from this world, but thou art not the only one; [death] cometh to all. Do not cling, in fondness and weakness, to this life. Even though thou clingest out of weakness, thou hast not the power to remain here. Thou wilt gain nothing more than wandering in this *Samsāra*.[9] Be not attached [to this world]; be not weak. Remember the Precious Trinity.[10]

O nobly-born, whatever fear and terror may come to thee in the *Chönyid Bardo*, forget not these words; and, bearing their meaning at heart, go forwards: in them lieth the vital secret of recognition:

Alas! when the Uncertain Experiencing of Reality is dawning upon me here,

With every thought of fear or terror or awe for all [apparitional appearances] set aside,

May I recognize whatever [visions] appear, as the reflections of mine own consciousness;

May I know them to be of the nature of apparitions in the Bardo:

When at this all-important moment [of opportunity] of achieving a great end,

May I not fear the bands of Peaceful and Wrathful [Deities], mine own thought-forms.

Repeat thou these [verses] clearly, and remembering their significance as thou repeatest them, go forwards, [O nobly-born]. Thereby, whatever visions of awe or terror appear, recognition is certain; and forget not this vital secret art lying therein.

O nobly-born, when thy body and mind were separating, thou must have experienced a glimpse of the Pure Truth, subtle, sparkling, bright dazzling, glorious, and radiantly awesome, in appearance like a mirage moving across a landscape in spring-time in one continuous stream of vibrations. Be not daunted thereby, nor terrified, nor awed. That is the radiance of thine own true nature. Recognize it.

From the midst of that radiance, the natural sound of Reality, reverberating like a thousand thunders simultaneously sounding, will come. That is the natural sound of thine own real self. Be not daunted thereby, nor terrified, nor awed.

Death and the Intermediate State

The body, which thou hast now is called the thought-body of propensities.[11] Since thou hast not a material body of flesh and blood, whatever may come,—sounds, lights, or rays,—are, all three, unable to harm thee: thou art incapable of dying. It is quite sufficient for thee to know that these apparitions are thine own thought-forms. Recognize this to be the *Bardo*.

O nobly-born, if thou dost not now recognize thine own thought-forms, whatever of meditation or of devotion thou mayest have performed while in the human world—if thou hast not met with this present teaching—the lights will daunt thee, the sounds will awe thee, and the rays will terrify thee. Shouldst thou not know this all-important key to the teachings,—not being able to recognize the sounds, lights, and rays,—thou wilt have to wander in the *Samsāra*.

Notes

1 The 'nerve-centres' are the 'psychic centres' (*cakra*). The 'nerve-centre of wisdom' is located in the heart-centre (*anāhata-cakra*).
2 'Knower,' i.e. the mind in its knowing functions.
3 The mind in its natural, or primal, state.
4 That is, the 'psychic nerves,' *pingāla-nādī* and *idā-nādī*.
5 *Brāhmarandhra*, the fissure on the top of the cranium identified with *sutura frontalis*.
6 From the union of the two states of mind, or consciousness, is born the state of Perfect Enlightenment, Buddhahood. The Dharma-Kāya ('Body of Truth') symbolizes the purest and the highest state of being, a state of supramundane consciousness.
7 The references are (1) to the share of food being set aside for the deceased during the funeral rites; (2) to his corpse being prepared for the shroud; (3) to his bed or sleeping-place.
8 The *Chönyid Bardo* is the intermediate state during the experiencing of Reality. The *Sidpa Bardo* represents the state wherein the deceased is seeking rebirth.
9 *Samsāra*, the universal becoming.
10 That is, the Buddha, the Dharma (=the Law, the Doctrine), the Samgha (the entire community of monks and hermits).
11 'Thought-body' or 'mind-body' born of the past worldly existence.

W. Y. Evans-Wentz (translator and editor), *The Tibetan Book of the Dead* (Oxford, 3rd ed.; 1957), pp. 90-2, 95-7, 101-4

C. FUNERARY RITUALS

163. 'AFFORD HIM EASY ACCESS, EARTH': A VEDIC FUNERARY HYMN

('Rig Veda,' X, 18)

1. Go hence, O Death,[1] pursue thy special pathway
   apart from that which gods are wont to travel.
   To thee I say it who hast eyes and hearest: touch
   not our offspring, injure not our heroes.
2. As ye have come effacing Mrityu's footstep,[2] to
   farther times prolonging your existence,
   May ye be rich in children and possessions, cleansed,
   purified, and meet for sacrificing.
3. Divided from the dead are these, the living: now
   is our calling on the gods successful
   We have come forth for dancing and for laughter,
   to farther times prolonging our existence.
4. Here I erect this rampart for the living; let none
   of these, none other reach this limit.
   May they survive a hundred lengthened autumns,
   and may they bury Death beneath this mountain.[3]
5. As the days follow days in close succession, as with
   the seasons duly come the seasons,
   As each successor fails not his foregoer, so form the
   lives of these, O great Ordainer[4]
6. Live your full lives and find old age delightful, all of
   you striving one behind the other.[5]
   May Tvashtar,[6] maker of fair things, be gracious,
   and lengthen out the days of your existence.
7. Let these unwidowed dames with noble husbands
   adorn themselves with fragrant balm and unguent.
   Decked with fair jewels, tearless, free from sorrow,
   first let the wives ascend unto the place.[7]

8. Rise, come unto the world of life, O woman: come
     he is lifeless by whose side thou liest.
   Wifehood with this thy husband was thy portion,
     who took thy hand and wooed thee as a lover.[8]

9. From his dead hand I take the bow he carried, that
     it may be our power and might and glory.
   There art thou, there; and here with noble heroes
     may we o'ercome all hosts that fight against us.

10. Betake thee[9] to the lap of the earth the mother, of earth
     far-spreading, very kind and gracious.
   Young dame, wool-soft unto the guerdon-giver, may
     she preserve thee from Destruction's bosom.

11. Heave thyself, Earth, nor press thee downward
     heavily: afford him easy access, gently tending him.
   Earth, as a mother wraps her skirt about her child,
     so cover him.

12. Now let the heaving earth be free from motion: yea,
     let a thousand clods remain above him.
   Be they to him a home distilling fatness, here let
     them ever be his place of refuge.

13. I stay the earth from thee, while over thee I place
     this piece of earth. May I be free from injury.
   Here let the Fathers keep this pillar firm for thee,
     and there let Yama make thee an abiding place.[10]

14. Even as an arrow's feathers, they have laid me down
     at day's decline.
   My parting speech have I drawn back as 'twere a
     courser with the rein.

Notes

1 Mrityu, a personification of death, while Yama (see stanza 13 below) is the god who rules the spirits of the departed.

2 I.e., 'losing' Death by erasing his tracks and frustrating his approach. The stanza is addressed to those assembled for the funeral rites.

3 Having absolved the living from impurity (stanza 2), the *adhvaryu* priest now raises a stone or earth mound, likened to a 'mountain,' to further bar the path of Death and to limit his domain.

4 Dhātar, a divine being who is creator, arranger and maintainer of all things, and who is particularly associated with matrimony and fertility.

5 Human lives should succeed one another, with their ideal 'hundred autumns' each, in as orderly a fashion as the seasons.

6 The divine artisan, shaper of forms; a god celebrated for his generative powers.

7 At this point the women now go up to the raised 'place' (*yoni*, a word which also means 'womb,' 'place of origin'), where the corpse lies with his widow beside him.

8 This stanza is addressed to the widow, either by the priest or by the husband's brother, as she is summoned to return to the realm of the living. (The levirate marriage is mentioned elsewhere in *Rig Veda*, x, e.g. 40.2).

9 The deceased.

10 After the committal of the body to the earth the priest has perhaps placed a beam or lid across the grave to 'stay the earth' and make the bodily resting place as secure as that which Yama provides for the spirit in the other world. This priestly act is cautious, nonetheless, as 'injury' may accrue from contact with the impurity of death. Stanza 14 is obviously a later addition.

Translation by Ralph T. H. Griffith, in his *The Hymns of the Rigveda*, IV (Benares, 1892), pp. 137-9; adapted by M. Eliade

164. THE AZTEC FUNERARY RITUAL (BERNARDINO DE SAHAGÚN)

When among the Aztecs a mortal died the 'straw death,' before the corpse the priest uttered these words: 'Our son, thou art finished with the sufferings and fatigues of this life. It hath pleased our Lord to take thee hence, for thou hast not eternal life in this world; our existence is as a ray of the sun. He hath given thee the grace of knowing us and of associating in our common life. Now the god Mictlantecutli and the goddess Mictecaciuatl [Lord and Lady of Hell] have made thee to share their abode. We shall all follow thee, for it is our destiny, and the abode is broad enough to receive the whole world. Thou wilt be heard of no longer among us. Behold, thou art gone to the domain of darkness, where there is neither light nor window. Neither shalt thou come hither again, nor needst thou concern thyself for thy return, for thine absence is eternal. Thou dost leave thy children poor and orphaned, not knowing what will be their end nor how they will support the fatigues of this life. As for us, we shall not delay to go to join thee there where thou wilt be.' Then upon the head of the body, like another baptism, the priest let fall a few drops of water and beside it placed a bowl of water: 'Lo, the water of which in this life thou hast made use; this for thy journey.' And like another Book of the Dead, in due order certain papers were laid upon the mummy-form corpse: 'Lo, with this thou shalt pass the two clashing mountains. . . . With this thou shalt pass the road where the serpent awaiteth thee. . . . With this thou shalt pass the lair of the green lizard. . . .

Lo, wherewith thou shalt cross the eight deserts. . . . And the eight hills. . . . And behold with what thou canst traverse the place of the winds that drive with obsidian knives.' Thus the perils of the Underworld Way were to be passed, and the soul to arrive before Mictlantecutli, whence after four years he should fare onward until, by the aid of his dog, sacrificed at his grave, he should pass over the Ninefold Stream, and thence, hound with master, enter into the eternal house of the dead, Chicomemictlan, the Ninth Hell.

> H. B. Alexander, *The World's Rim* (Lincoln, Neb.: University of Nebraska Press, 1953), pp. 201-2; translating and summarizing Bernardino de Sahagún, *Historia de las Cosas de la Nueva España* bk. III, App. I

165. FUNERARY RITES OF THE TORADJA
(CENTRAL CELEBES)

The Toradja had two funerals, which were separated by a considerable length of time. At the first of these the bodies were placed in temporary huts outside the village; at the second the bones were cleaned and given a definitive burial in caves.

Lamentations for the dead person began the moment he expired. They were always improvised, but stereotyped: it was said how much he was missed, he was asked why the mourners couldn't have gone in his place and his virtues were summed up. For many of the mourners, at least, it was a purely formal affair, unconnected with feelings of affection for the dead person. Many young girls, it would seem, participated merely to show off their voices. Men hardly took part in it and some were even quite annoyed by it.

The corpse was laid out soon after death, preferably by some one who fetched the bones for the second funeral *(tonggola)*, otherwise by an older member of the family. It was not washed, nor were its clothes usually removed, new and handsome ones being put on over the old ones or laid over the body. Cloths were bound about the knees, arms and around the head under the chin to make the body easier to carry and to keep the mouth from falling open. Now and then gold dust, a gold piece or beads (preferably white) were put into its mouth, supposedly as food for its *angga*.[1] In Pu'u-mboto they said on this occasion : 'Just as white as the beads will be the grain of the rice which you will give us. Do not come to us, in the guise of pigs, mice or rice birds; give us the grain (po'oe).' Sometimes beads were placed on the eyes, a small mirror on the chest and pieces of money on the cheeks and forehead.

A bit of hair and the nails of the dead person were cut off and made up into a package along with the knife used for this purpose. They were either carried about or kept in the house (presumably by the closest relative, though from other remarks it would seem that the hair and nails of much loved or admired persons were in great demand) for a long time—by some as long as six generations. During the first funeral, from the time the body was removed from the house until the *moombe ue* had been performed, this package served as a substitute for the dead person, a bit of everything one ate or chewed being placed beside it. Hair and nails were said to be kept 'so that his *tanoana*[2] will be transferred to us.' Many said that they allayed their longing for the dead, and others, 'We keep hair and nails in order not to forget the dead, and the dead will then bless us.' They were also used as medicine for the crops, and it was said that, 'if we didn't cut off the nails of the dead they would pinch off the rice ears with them or dig up the roots of the plants.' A widow would keep the hair of her dead husband 'so that his *tanoana* would not part from hers,' but would throw it away when she remarried.

Once the corpse was dressed it was laid on a mat in the most appropriate part of the house and a sort of canopy *(batuwali)* was built over it. The *batuwali* (the word probably once meant 'room') consisted of four bamboo posts with cross bars, covered with a piece of cotton or sleeping mat to form the roof, and with curtains hung from the cross bars. Pinang blossoms were hung from the posts and beads by the head of the corpse. Beside the body was a basket with sirih-pinang and an egg, which served as its food. The *batuwali* was further decorated with various cotton goods, some of which later accompanied the corpse as presents.

While the body remained in the house it was fed. The food was placed beside it and removed after an hour and given to a slave to eat. At some point or other during the proceedings a buffalo and a few pigs were killed, the former being intended to serve as a means of transportation to the underworld for its master. The house was always full of people, especially at night. A circle which could not be broken was formed around the *batuwali* in order to protect the dead person from witches or the souls of the dead. The hearth fire and a torch had, moreover, to be kept burning. The people keeping watch could not sleep for a moment, as this would not only endanger the corpse but their own *tanoana* could easily be seized and taken to the underworld. Round dances *(kajori, raego)* and certain singing games were prohibited during these nights, though various others were especially performed on these occasions. Chief among the latter were the *djondjo awa* and the *lina*, which formed the greatest attractions for the young people. The first of these consisted in reciting improvised couplets which were alternated with a refrain beginning with the words *djondjo awa*. Kruyt thought these words probably came from *nd'o'u-nd'o'u wawa,* meaning 'go, go, accompany him' or 'take him away,' referring to the dead person. The *lina* was a song (plaintively sung, each line of which ended with the meaningless word *lina*, which Kruyt thought came from *linga*, 'to sing,' but which the Toradja equated with *ine*, 'mother.' The two games were alternated. They were said to be performed to distract and console the *angga* now that it had to leave the earth, and in them the *angga* was first taken on a trip to another region and then conducted to the underworld, or, in at least one case, to Buju mpotumangi, 'the mountain of weeping,' where it was handed over to other souls of the dead who had come to meet it. When leave was taken from the *angga* it was asked not to take the *tanoana* of the rice and other plants with it to the underworld, which would make the crops fail. Throughout the *djondjo awa* and *lina* a man and a young girl carried on a conversation of a piquant nature. . . .

The coffin was called either *bangka* or *jumu*. The second of these was a general term meaning 'covering'; the first meant 'boat,' and was still used in Pu'u-mboto in this sense. That the coffin was indeed thought of as a boat is borne out by the fact that if one dreamed of somebody rowing in a boat it was assumed that that person would soon die. The coffin was hollowed out of a tree trunk split lengthwise to form a cover, called *lakinja*, 'the man,' and a receptacle, called *tinanja*, 'the woman.' Aside from the handles at either end which were sometimes carved in the form of animal heads (Kruyt had seen those of pigs and goats) and which supposedly had no particular significance, the coffins were not decorated. . . .

Before the coffin was removed from the house a shaman performed the *mowurake mpo'onto tanoana*, 'shaman's ritual to hold back the tanoana,' over the closest relatives, supposedly to keep their souls from following the coffin. They squatted down near it and were covered by a costly old cloth *(bana)*. The shaman then touched all the heads under the cloth and finally the coffin with a *rare* consisting of a young arenga palm leaf and small bell and a basket in which was a branch of cordyline. This she repeated seven times and then touched the corpse with it seven times from the feet to the head while reciting a litany. . . .

Unfortunately Kruyt did not record the litanies recited on these occasions, so it is impossible to be sure of their significance, but it would seem that in all the cases the purpose was to prepare the people for a hazardous journey. The funeral ceremony was performed according to Kruyt to keep the *tanoana* of the surviving close relatives from following the dead person, but as we shall see, they too were supposed to be in the underworld while in mourning, so it is possible that the ceremony served to prepare them for this trip. As the dead person was similarly treated with the *rare* it may also have been done with the same intention. This, at any rate, was the explanation given by the Toradja for the *montende rare* performed over the corpse of a shaman.

When removing the coffin and on the way to its temporary shelter outside the village everything was done to prevent the soul of the dead from finding its way back to its home, except in the case of people who had left no relatives of the same generation behind. It was removed through the window, or if it was too small a wall was taken out for this purpose, and sometimes (generally in the case of infants) it was let out through the floor. . . .

The small hut which served as temporary resting place for the corpse *(tambea)* was a pile construction erected a short distance to the north, south or west of the village. It was never built to the east of it, as the village would then lie in the path of the *angga*, which went to the west. Account was also taken of the prevailing wind, to reduce to a minimum the smell of the rotting corpse in the village. It was solidly built, with no walls and a low roof. The roof was laid on differently than in houses for the living and the notched tree trunk which served as a ladder was placed so that the steps faced downwards, as the dead saw everything reversed. Long bamboo poles, each with a piece of white cotton attached, were erected about the hut. . . .

Upon arrival the coffin was placed in the hut with the feet pointing west. A hole was made in the bottom in which a long bamboo was inserted which reached to the ground and served to drain off the juices of decomposition. Then (in Lage at any rate and also Kruyt presumed, elsewhere) the shaman performed a ritual to lure back the *tanoana* of family members which might have gotten into the coffin so that they would not be taken by the *angga* to the underworld. The cover was then placed on the coffin, which was bound about with rattan, eight times for men and nine for women. Finally the cracks between the two parts were filled with fungus and covered with strips of bark cloth. A sleeping mat, a food basket, a cooking pot, the dead person's sirih pouch and sword and a few other articles and food were either hung from or laid on the roof of the hut.

Somewhat different customs were observed with respect to the corpse of a shaman. According to Kruyt these were to be explained by the fact that the soul (angga) of a shaman did not go to the underworld (Torate), but to Mungku mpe'anta-anta, 'the mountain which serves as resting place,' in 'the land of the wurake spirits in the sky.' This was supposed to be where the roads from the upper and underworlds came together. Unfortunately, however, in the litany which Kruyt quoted in this connection her soul was spoken of as going to Nanggi or Linduju, both names for the underworld. Supposedly to demonstrate that her 'soul' went to heaven a small bamboo was placed in her mouth as a blow pipe through which she blew her 'breath' (inosa) to the sky. As we have seen, however, inosa is 'life force' and is closely akin to tanoana, thus quite different from angga. The ceremony by which, according to Kruyt, the shaman's soul was brought to heaven was called montende rare, 'to toss up the rare.' According to the Toradja it served 'to equip the dead person's angga (for its trip).' . . .

A hen or rooster, depending on whether or not the dead person was female or male respectively, was also tied to the hut or coffin. . . .

For the corpse of an important person a slave was designated as tandojae; at least that was the case in Onda'e, Lage and Lamusa according to the first edition of Kruyt and Adriani. He slept in the hut at night and kept a torch burning, and in the daytime he kept the flies away and wiped up the liquids from the corpse. His main duty was to prevent witches from 'eating up' the body. He could talk to no one and took his food where he could find it. . . .

After the coffin had been deposited in the hut leave was taken from the dead person. There was no set formula for this, though the sentiments expressed were apparently always pretty much the same. For example, 'O father (mother), we have put everything for you down here. Stay here. Your (dead) relatives are coming to keep you company, and among them is also so and so, who will tell you what you must do and not do. As for us, whom you have left, we too have some one whose orders we obey.' This is the end of our relationship. This far you have a claim on us as your children. We are making the steps of your house black. Do not come back to us.' 'Here you have your food. Give us rain so that our rice will succeed, and give us dry weather so that we can burn the wood on our fields. Do not let any rice birds loose on us, or mice or pigs.' Later on people returned from time to time, however, to bring food for the *angga (melo'a)*, as, for example, when people were called together to work in the fields *(mesale)*. Otherwise the dead would come to fetch it themselves.

Although official leave had been taken from the dead person his soul was still thought to return to visit the living, especially the first night after the disposal of the coffin, and for this reason the *batuwali* was left standing for eight nights (for a man) or nine nights (for a woman) after his death. If it was broken up earlier the sleeping mat was left for this length of time. Torch and hearth fire were kept burning and wirih and food were placed by its side. The shaman was helpful in preventing these visits, as she could see the *angga*. On this first night after the removal of the corpse she also descended to the underworld to fetch the *tanoana* of the relatives which might have followed the soul of the dead person there, and eight days after the removal (for a man; nine days after for a woman) she performed a ceremony with the aid of the *wurake* to rescue the *angga* from the juices of its decomposing corpse *(moombe ue)*. . . .

Aside from the general mourning there were special restrictions for a widow or widower. Until the body had been removed she (unless otherwise stated what follows applied equally to widows and widowers) remained by its head with a female companion of her family, who mourned for her, at its foot. A man likewise shared the mourning with a male member of the family (around the *Lake* a widow had eight companions and a widower nine). When the body was removed she was surrounded by rain mats and pieces of bark cloth, forming a small cubicle in which she remained as a rule for three days, sometimes less, 'in any case until the shaman had finished her work. . . .

In the case of the death of an important person, however, mourning was not ended until a head had been taken for him. Till then the mourners could put on no new clothes or take sirih from another's pouch, nor could coconuts be taken from the trees. If the village was at war then a head was taken from the enemy; otherwise a slave or somebody suspected of witchcraft or sorcery was bought from another village, brought home and cut to pieces. The person who had contributed most toward his purchase gave the first blow, holding onto the victim's hair, and he also took the head. The mourning could also be ended with a head taken by another tribe if necessary. The close relatives of the dead person were responsible for getting the head or sacrificial victim. A widower would not dare return until he had got one by some means or other, even if it took three years or longer. . . .

At the ceremonies ending the mourning the widow was told not to stay in the underworld, as she had been freed from the mourning restrictions by victory. The poles around the hut in which the coffin rested were cut down and a piece of the scalp of the victim was inserted in a notch in one of the handles of the coffin. Then the dead person was calmed by singing to him: 'Lie down again dead one, in the abode of the dead *(Nanggi)* is the resting place of your soul.' Then everybody returned to the village, where the clothes of the widow or widower were cut through and the mourning was declared to be ended. The leader of the troop of head-hunters cut a notch in the ridge pole on the east side of the house and inserted a piece of scalp in it, and then everybody repaired to the temple, where an old man addressed the dead person for whom the mourning had just been ended: 'Do not come to us in the form of mice or pigs, because we have mourned your death. From now on we will be happy: we will play the drums and sing; you see to it that our rice succeeds.' After a few strokes on the drum he continued: 'Any one who has anything to claim from others may demand payment from the debtor; he who wants to set out against the enemy or wants to marry let him go ahead, for the mourning period is over.'

After some time a second funeral was held for the bones of the dead. How soon this was done depended on various circumstances. In the first place a plentiful harvest was necessary because of the enormous amounts of food consumed, and for this reason was usually celebrated shortly after it. This had the further advantage that there was sufficient free time for it. It could not be celebrated every year in each village, however, because of the high cost, so either a village waited a few years until there were enough dead to make it worth while, or did it jointly with one or more villages. If there was no opportunity for holding a regular funeral, and certain signs, such as sickness or a plague of mice, made it urgent, then an emergency feast was organized which lasted only one day and to which no guests were invited. . . .

About eleven in the morning of the first day the bones were fetched by the bone collectors *(tonggola),* roughly sorted out and made up into packages. When they returned to the village one of the oldest female *tonggola* treated everybody who felt the least bit sick with one of the skulls. After this the bones were brought to the feast grounds where the male *tonggola* slaughtered a tethered buffalo. . . .

33

Death, Afterlife, Eschatology

The souls of the people whose bones had been assembled were brought from the underworld by the shamans. At the *mompemate* there was no prescribed number of them, but at the *motengke* there had to be five plus two male assistants. The litany described how the dead were waked, dressed themselves and were conducted through the underworld to the pinang tree which they climbed to reach the earth, where they came out in Mori (to the east of the Toradja), and finally were led to the temple or feast hut. There they were welcomed by their relatives and entertained by them and the rest of the participants with singing and dancing. In the songs the dead were brought up to date on the current affairs of the living. During this part of the ceremonies, which lasted a whole night from dusk to dawn, the men were permitted to ask a girl to be their partner. The man rested his elbow on the girl's shoulder and was allowed to touch her face and breast, in exchange for which he gave her a sarong or some other present. When she had had enough of it she would hang a white cotton or bark cloth sarong over his shoulder and the relationship would be ended. While they were together they were considered to be man and wife.

The next day the *angga* were conducted by the shamans to their final resting place.

Notes

1 Ghost; personality of a dead person.
2 The spiritual part of man.

R. E. Downs, *The Religion of the Bare'e Speaking Toradja of Central Celebes* (The Hague: Uitgeverij Excelsior, 1956), pp. 77-89; summarizing N. Adriani and A. C. Kruyt

D. EGYPTIAN CONCEPTIONS OF DEATH

166. THE DEAD PHARAOH ASCENDS TO HEAVEN

(From the 'Pyramid Texts')

The so-called Pyramid Texts *are religious texts inscribed on the interior walls of the pyramids of certain pharaohs of the fifth and sixth dynasties (ca. 2425-2300 B.C.). The* Pyramid Texts *contain the oldest references to Egyptian cosmology and theology, but they are primarily concerned with the victorious passage of the dead pharaoh to his new, celestial abode.*

Thy two wings are spread out like a falcon with thick plumage, like the hawk seen in the evening traversing the sky *(Pyr. § 1048)*.

He flies who flies; this king Pepi flies away from you, ye mortals. He is not of the earth, he is of the sky. . . . This king Pepi flies as a cloud to the sky, like a masthead bird; this king Pepi kisses the sky like a falcon, this king Pepi reaches the sky like Horizon-god (Harakhte) (Pyr. § 890-1).

Thou ascendest to the sky as a falcon, thy feathers are (those of) geese (Pyr. § 913).

King Unis goes to the sky, king Unis goes to the sky! On the wind! On the wind! (Pyr. § 309).

Stairs to the sky are laid for him that he may ascend thereon to the sky (Pyr. § 365).

King Unis ascends upon the ladder which his father Re (the Sun-god) made for him (Pyr. § 390).

Atum has done that which he said he would do for this king Pepi II, binding for him the rope-ladder, joining together the (wooden) ladder for this king Pepi II; (thus) this king is far from the abomination of men (Pyr. § 2083).

'How beautiful to see, how satisfying to behold,' say the gods, 'when this god (meaning the king) ascends to the sky. His fearfulness is on his head, his terror is at his side, his magical charms are before him.' Geb has done for him as was done for himself (Geb). The gods and souls of Buto, the gods and souls of Hierakonpolis, the gods in the sky and the gods on earth come to him. They make supports for king Unis on their arms. Thou ascendest, O King Unis, to the sky. Ascend upon it in this its name 'Ladder' (Pyr. § 476-9).

[*Over and over again we find the assurance that the double doors of the sky are opened before the pharaoh.*]

Opened are the double doors of the horizon; unlocked are its bolts (Pyr. § 194; n.b. this is a constant refrain in the Pyramid Texts; cf. § 603, 604, 1408, etc).

[*The King's heralds hasten to announce his advent to the Sun god.*]

Thy messengers go, thy swift messengers run, thy heralds make haste. They announce to Re that thou hast come, (even) this king Pepi (§ 1539-40).

This king Pepi found the gods standing, wrapped in their garments, their white sandals on their feet. They cast off their white sandals to the earth, they throw off their garments. 'Our heart was not glad until thy coming,' say they (Pyr. § 1197).

[*More often the gods themselves proclaim the pharaoh's coming.*]

O Re-Atum! This king Unis comes to thee, an imperishable glorious-one, lord of the affairs of the place of the four pillars (the sky). Thy son comes to thee. This king Unis comes to thee (Pyr. Ut. 217).

[*The dead pharaoh boldly approaches the Sun god with the words:*]

I, O Re, am this one of whom thou didst say . . . 'My son!' My father are thou, O Re. . . . Behold king Pepi, O Re. This king Pepi is thy son. . . . This king Pepi shines in the east like Re, he goes in the west like Kheprer. This king Pepi lives on what whereon Horus (son of Re) lord of the sky lives, by command of Horus lord of the sky' (Pyr. § 886-8).

The king ascends to the sky among the gods dwelling in the sky. He stands on the great [dais], he hears (in judicial session) the (legal) affairs of men. Re finds thee upon the shores of the sky in this lake that is in Nut (the Sky-goddess). 'The arriver comes!' say the gods. He (Re) gives thee his arm on the stairway to the sky. 'He who knows his place comes,' say the gods. O Pure One, assume thy throne in the barque of Re and sail thou the sky. . . . Sail thou with the Imperishable Stars, sail thou with the Unwearied Stars. Receive thou the 'tribute' of the Evening Barque, become thou a spirit dwelling in Dewat. Live thou this pleasant life which the lord of the horizon lives (*Pyr.* § 1169-72).

Translation by J. H. Breasted, in his *Development of Religion and Thought in Ancient Egypt* (Chicago, 1912), pp. 109-15, 118-20, 122, 136

167. THE DEAD PHARAOH BECOMES OSIRIS

(From the 'Pyramid Texts')

A great number of Pyramid Texts present the different phases of the ritual assimilation of the dead pharaoh with Osiris.

As he (Osiris) lives, this king Unis lives; as he dies not, this king Unis dies not; as he perishes not, this king Unis perishes not (*Pyr. Ut.* 219).

[*The dead pharaoh receives the throne of Osiris, and becomes, like him, king of the dead.*]

Ho! king Neferkere (Pepi II)! How beautiful is this! How beautiful is this, which thy father Osiris has done for thee! He has given thee his throne, thou rulest those of the hidden places (the dead), thou leadest their august ones, all the glorious ones follow thee (*Pyr.* § 2022-3).

Translation by J. H. Breasted in his *Development of Religion and Thought in Ancient Egypt* (Chicago, 1912), pp. 145-6

168. OSIRIS—THE PROTOTYPE OF EVERY SOUL WHO HOPES TO CONQUER DEATH

('Coffin Texts,' I, 197)

The so-called Coffin Texts, inscribed on the interior of coffins, belong to the Middle Kingdom (2250-1580 B.C.). They attest a marked 'democratization' of the ancient funerary ritual of the pharaoh. Just as the pharaoh of earlier times had claimed to participate in the fate of Osiris, so each soul now hoped to achieve a ritual assimilation to the god.

Now are you a king's son, a prince,
as long as your soul exists, so long will your heart be with you.
Anubis is mindful of you in Busiris,
your soul rejoices in Abydos where your body is happy on the High Hill.
Your embalmer rejoices in every place.
Ah, truly, you are the chosen one!
you are made whole in this your dignity which is before me,
Anubis' heart is happy over the work of his hands
and the heart of the Lord of the Divine Hall is thrilled
when he beholds this good god,
Master of those that have been and Ruler over those that are to come.

Translation by R. T. Rundle Clark, in his *Myth and Symbol in Ancient Egypt* (London, 1960), p. 134

See also nos. 88, 109

169. SURVIVAL AS BA AND SURVIVAL IN THE TOMB ARE COMPLEMENTARY

Thou shalt come in and go out, thy heart rejoicing, in the favour of the Lord of the Gods, a good burial [being thine] after a venerable old age, when age has come, thou assuming thy place in the coffin, and joining earth on the high ground of the west.

Thou shalt change into a living Ba[1] and surely he will have power to obtain bread and water and air; and thou shalt take shape as a heron or swallow, as a falcon or a bittern, whichever thou pleasest.

Thou shalt cross in the ferryboat and shalt not turn back, thou shalt sail on the waters of the flood, and thy life shall start afresh. Thy Ba shall not depart from thy corpse and thy Ba shall become divine with the blessed dead. The perfect Ba's shall speak to thee, and thou shalt be an equal amongst them in receiving what is given on earth. Thou shalt have power over water, shalt inhale air, and shalt be surfeited with the desires of thy heart. Thine eyes shall be given to thee so as to see, and thine ears so as to hear, thy mouth speaking, and thy feet walking. Thy arms and thy shoulders shall move for thee, thy flesh shall be firm, thy muscles shall be easy and thou shalt exult in all thy limbs. Thou shalt examine thy body and find it whole and sound, no ill whatever adhering to thee. Thine own true heart shall be with thee, yea, thou shalt have thy former heart. Thou shalt go up to the sky, and shalt penetrate the Netherworld in all forms that thou likes.

Note

1 The dead man conceived as living an animated existence after death was called Ba. . . . The word Ba means 'animation, manifestation.'

> Translation by A. Gardiner, *The Attitude of the Ancient Egyptians to Death and the Dead* (Cambridge, Eng., 1935), pp. 29-30; as quoted in Henri Frankfort, *Ancient Egyptian Religion* (New York: Columbia University Press, 1948)

170. THE EGYPTIAN LAND OF SILENCE AND DARKNESS

In this song a woman laments the death of her husband.

How sad is the descent in the Land of Silence. The wakeful sleeps, he who did not slumber at night lies still forever. The scorners say: The dwelling-place of the inhabitants of the West is deep and dark. It has no door, no window, no light to illuminate it, no north wind to refresh the heart. The sun does not rise there, but they lie every day in darkness. . . . The guardian has been taken away to the Land of Infinity.

Those who are in the West are cut off, and their existence is misery; one is loathe to go to join them. One cannot recount one's experiences but one rests in one place of eternity in darkness.

> Translation by Henri Frankfort (after Kees), in Frankfort, *Ancient Egyptian Religion* (New York: Columbia University Press, 1948)

E. THE ROADS TO THE NETHER WORLD

171. THE INITIATES IN THE ORPHIC-PYTHAGOREAN BROTHERHOOD ARE TAUGHT THE ROAD TO THE LOWER WORLD

(The Funerary Gold Plates)

[Plate from Petelia, South Italy, fourth-third century B.C.]

Thou shalt find to the left of the House of Hades a spring,
And by the side thereof standing a white cypress.
To this spring approach not near.
But thou shalt find another, from the Lake of Memory
Cold water flowing forth, and there are guardians before it.
Say, 'I am a child of Earth and starry Heaven;
But my race is of Heaven (alone). This ye know yourselves.
But I am parched with thirst and I perish. Give me quickly
The cold water flowing forth from the Lake of Memory.'
And of themselves they will give thee to drink of the holy spring,
And thereafter among the other heroes thou shalt have lordship.

[Plate from Eleuthernai in Crete, second century B.C.]

I am parched with thirst and I perish—Nay, drink of me (or, But give
   me to drink of)
The ever-flowing spring on the right, where the cypress is.
Who art thou? . . .
Whence art thou?—I am the son of Earth and starry Heaven.

[Plate from Thurii, South Italy, fourth-third century B.C.]

But so soon as the spirit hath left the light of the sun,
Go to the right as far as one should go, being right wary in all things.
Hail, thou who hast suffered the suffering. This thou hadst never
   suffered before.
Thou art become god from man.
A kid thou art fallen into milk.

Hail, hail to thee journeying the right hand road
By holy meadows and groves of Persephone.

[Three more tablets from Thurii, of roughly the same date as the previous one.]

I come from the pure, pure Queen of those below,
And Eukles and Eubuleus, and other Gods and Daemons:
For I also avow that I am of your blessed race.
And I have paid the penalty for deeds unrighteous,
Whether it be that Fate laid me low or the gods immortal
Or . . . with star-flung thunderbolt.
I have flown out of the sorrowful, weary circle.
I have passed with swift feet to the diadem desired.
I have sunk beneath the bosom of the Mistress, the Queen of the
   underworld.
And now I come a suppliant to holy Persephoneia,
That of her grace she send men to the seats of the Hallowed.
Happy and blessed one, thou shalt be god instead of mortal.
A kid I have fallen into milk.

> Translation by W. K. C. Guthrie, in his *Orpheus and Greek Religion* (London, 1935), pp. 172-3

See also nos. 148-55

172. THE IRANIAN AFTERLIFE: THE CROSSING OF THE CINVAT BRIDGE AND THE ROADS TO HEAVEN AND HELL

('Mēnōk i Khrat,' I, 71-122)

According to Zoroastrian belief, the soul of the departed hovers near the body for three days. On the fourth day he faces a judgement on the 'Bridge of the Requiter' (Cinvat Bridge), where Rashn 'the righteous' impartially weighs his good and evil deeds. If the good actions preponderate over the evil ones, the soul is permitted to ascend to Heaven; if, on the contrary, there is a predominance of evil acts, it is dragged off to Hell. But for the Zoroastrians, Hell is not eternal. At the Last Judgement, at the end of time, the bodies are resurrected and reunited with their souls. Then there is a final and universal purgation, from *which all men without exception emerge spotless, and enter into Paradise.*

(71) Put not your trust in life, for at the last death must overtake you; (72) and dog and bird will rend your corpse and your bones will be tumbled on the earth. (73) For three days and nights the soul sits beside the pillow of the body. (74) And on the fourth day at dawn (the soul) accompanied by the blessed Srōsh, the good Vāy, and the mighty Vahrām, and opposed by Astvihāt (the demon of death), the evil Vāy, the demon Frēhzisht and the demon Vizisht, and pursued by the active ill-will of Wrath, the evil-doer who bears a bloody spear, (will reach) the lofty and awful Bridge of the Requiter to which every man whose soul is saved and every man whose soul is damned must come. Here does many an enemy lie in wait. (75) Here (the soul will suffer) from the ill-will of Wrath who wields a bloody spear and from Astvihāt who swallows all creation yet knows no sating, (76) and it will (benefit by) the mediation of Hihr, Srōsh, and Rashn, and will (needs submit) to the weighing (of his deeds) by the righteous Rashn who lets the scales of the spiritual gods incline to neither side, neither for the saved nor yet for the damned, nor yet for kings and princes: (77) not so much as a hair's breadth does he allow (the scales) to tip, and he is no respecter (of persons), (78) for he deals out impartial justice both to kings and princes and to the humblest of men.

(79) And when the soul of the saved passes over that bridge, the breadth of the bridge appears to be one parasang broad. (80) And the soul of the saved passes on accompanied by the blessed Srōsh. (81) And his own good deeds come to meet him in the form of a young girl, more beautiful and fair than any girl on earth. (82) And the soul of the saved says, 'Who art thou, for I have never seen a young girl on earth more beautiful or fair than thee.' (83) In answer the form of the young girl replies, 'I am no girl but thy own good deeds, O young man whose thoughts and words, deeds and religion were good: (84) for when on earth thou didst see one who offered sacrifice to the demons, then didst thou sit (apart) and offer sacrifice to the gods. (85) And when thou didst see a man do violence and rapine, afflict good men and treat them with contumely, and hoard up goods wrongfully obtained, then didst thou refrain from visiting creatures with violence and rapine of thine own; (86) (nay rather,) thou wast considerate to good men, didst entertain them and offer them hospitality, and give alms both to the man who came from near and to him who came from afar; (87) and thou didst amass thy wealth in righteousness. (88) And

when thou didst see one who passed a false judgement or took bribes or bore false witness, thou didst sit thee down and speak witness right and true. (89) I am thy good thoughts, good words, and good deeds which thou didst think and say and do. . . .'

(91) And when the soul departs from thence, then is a fragrant breeze wafted towards him,—(a breeze) more fragrant than any perfume. (92) Then does the soul of the saved ask Srōsh saying, 'What breeze is this, the like of which in fragrance I never smelt on earth?' (93) Then does the blessed Srōsh make answer to the soul of the saved, saying, 'This is a wind (wafted) from Heaven; hence is it so fragrant.'

(94) Then with his first step he bestrides (the heaven of) good thoughts, with his second (the heaven of) good words, and with his third (the heaven of) good deeds; and with his fourth step he reaches the Endless Light where is all bliss. (95) And all the gods and Amahraspands come to greet him and ask him how he has fared, saying, 'How was thy passage from those transient, fearful worlds where there is much evil to these worlds which do not pass away and in which there is no adversary, O young man whose thoughts and words, deeds and religion are good?'

(96) Then Ohrmazd, the Lord, speaks, saying, 'Do not ask him how he has fared, for he has been separated from his beloved body and has travelled on a fearsome road.' (97) And they served him with the sweetest of all foods even with the butter of early spring so that his soul may take its ease after the three nights terror of the Bridge inflicted on him by Astvihāt and the other demons, (98) and he is sat upon a throne everywhere bejewelled. . . . (100) And for ever and ever he dwells with the spiritual gods in all bliss for evermore.

(101) But when the man who is damned dies, for three days and nights does his soul hover near his head and weeps, saying, 'Whither shall I go and in whom shall I now take refuge?' (102) And during those three days and nights he sees with his eyes all the sins and wickedness that he committed on earth. (103) On the fourth day the demon Vizarsh comes and binds the soul of the damned in most shameful wise, and despite the opposition of the blessed Srōsh drags it off to the Bridge of the Requiter. (104) Then the righteous Rashn makes clear to the soul of the damned that it is damned (indeed).

(105) Then the demon Vizarsh seizes upon the soul of the damned, smites it and ill-treats it without pity, urged on by Wrath. (106) And the soul of the damned cries out with a loud voice, makes moan, and in supplication makes many a piteous plea; much does he struggle though his life-breath endures no more. (107) When all his struggling

and his lamentations have proved of no avail, no help is proffered him by any of the gods nor yet by any of the demons, but the demon Vizarsh drags him off against his will into nethermost Hell.

(108) Then a young girl who yet has no semblance of a young girl, comes to meet him. (109) And the soul of the damned says to that ill-favoured wench, 'Who art thou? for I have never seen an ill-favoured wench on earth more ill-favoured and hideous than thee.' (110) And in reply that ill-favoured wench says to him, 'I am no wench, but I am thy deeds,—hideous deeds,—evil thoughts, evil words, evil deeds, and an evil religion. (111) For when on earth thou didst see one who offered sacrifice to the gods, then didst thou sit (apart) and offer sacrifice to the demons. (112) And when thou didst see one who entertained good men and offered them hospitality, and gave alms both to those who came from near and to those who came from afar, then didst thou treat good men with contumely and show them dishonour, thou gavest them no alms and didst shut thy door (upon them). (113) And when thou didst see one who passed a just judgement or took no bribes or bore true witness or spoke up in righteousness, then didst thou sit down and pass false judgement, bear false witness, and speak unrighteously. . . .

(116) Then with his first step he goes to (the hell of) evil thoughts, with his second to (the hell of) evil words, and with his third to (the hell of) evil deeds. And with his fourth step he lurches into the presence of the accursed Destructive Spirit and the other demons. (117) And the demons mock at him and hold him up to scorn, saying, 'What grieved thee in Ohrmazd, the Lord, and the Amahraspands and in fragrant and delightful Heaven, and what grudge or complaint hadst thou of them that thou shouldst come to see Ahriman and the demons and murky Hell? for we will torment thee nor shall we have any mercy on thee, and for a long time shalt thou suffer torment.'

(118) And the Destructive Spirit cries out to the demons, saying, 'Ask not concerning him, for he has been separated from his beloved body, and has come through that most evil passage-way; (119) but serve him (rather) with the filthiest and most foul food that Hell can produce.'

(120) Then they bring him poison and venom, snakes and scorpions and other noxious reptiles (that flourish) in Hell, and they serve him with these to eat. (121) And until the Resurrection and the Final Body he must remain in Hell, suffering much torment and many kinds

of chastisement. (122) And the food that he must for the most part eat there is all, as it were, putrid and like unto blood.

Mēnōk i Khrat, edited by Anklesaria. Translation by R. C. Zaehner, in his *The Teachings of the Magi* (London, 1956), pp. 133-8

173. A SIBERIAN (GOLDI) FUNERARY CEREMONY: THE SHAMAN GUIDES THE SOUL TO THE UNDERWORLD

The Goldi have two funerary ceremonies: the *nimgan*, which takes place seven days or even longer (two months) after the death, and the *kazatauri*, the great ceremony celebrated some time after the former and at the end of which the soul is conducted to the underworld. During the *nimgan* the shaman enters the dead person's house with his drum, searches for the soul, captures it, and makes it enter a sort of cushion (*fanya*). The banquet follows, participated in by all the relatives and friends of the dead person present in the *fanya*; the shaman offers the latter brandy. The *kazatauri* begins in the same way. The shaman dons his costume, takes his drum, and goes to search for the soul in the vicinity of the yurt. During all this time he dances and recounts the difficulties of the road to the underworld. Finally he captures the soul and brings it into the house, where he makes it enter the *fanya*. The banquet continues late into the night, and the food that is left over is thrown into the fire by the shaman. The women bring a bed into the yurt, the shaman puts the *fanya* in it, covers it with a blanket, and tells the dead person to sleep. He then lies down in the yurt and goes to sleep himself.

The following day he again dons his costume and wakes the deceased by drumming. Another banquet follows and at night (for the ceremony may continue for several days) he puts the *fanya* to bed again and covers it up. Finally one morning the shaman begins his song and, addressing the deceased, advises him to eat well but to drink sparingly, for the journey to the underworld is extremely difficult for the drunken person. At sunset preparations for the departure are made. The shaman sings, dances, and daubs his face with soot. He invokes his helping spirits and begs them to guide him and the dead man in the beyond. He leaves the yurt for a few minutes and climbs a notched tree that has been set up in readiness; from here he sees the road to the under-

45

world. (He has, in fact, climbed the World Tree and is at the summit of the world.) At the same time he sees many other things: plentiful snow, successful hunting and fishing, and so on.

Returning to the yurt, he summons two powerful tutelary spirits to help him; *butchu*, a kind of one-legged monster with a human face and feathers, and *koori*, a long-necked bird. Without the help of these two spirits, the shaman could not come back from the underworld; he makes the most difficult part of the return journey sitting on the *koori*'s back.

After shamanizing until he is exhausted, he sits down, facing the west, on a board that represents a Siberian sled. The *fanya*, containing the dead person's soul, and a basket of food are set beside him. The shaman asks the spirits to harness the dogs to the sled and for a 'servant' to keep him company during the journey. A few moments later he 'sets off' for the land of the dead.

The songs he intones and the words he exchanges with the 'servant' make it possible to follow his route. At first the road is easy, but the difficulties increase as the land of the dead is approached. A great river bars the way, and only a good shaman can get his team and sled across to the other bank. Some time later, he sees signs of human activity; footprints, ashes, bits of wood—the village of the dead is not far away. Now, indeed, dogs are heard barking at no great distance, the smoke from the yurts is seen, the first reindeer appear. The shaman and the deceased have reached the underworld. At once the dead gather and ask the shaman to tell them his name and that of the newcomer. The shaman is careful not to give his real name; he searches through the crowd of spirits for the close relatives of the soul he is conducting, so that he may entrust it to them. Having done so, he hastens to return to earth and, arriving, gives a long account of all that he has seen in the land of the dead and the impressions of the dead man whom he escorted. He brings each of the audience greetings from their dead relatives and even distributes little gifts from them. At the close of the ceremony the shaman throws the *fanya* into the fire. The strict obligations of the living to the dead are now terminated.

M. Eliade, *Shamanism: Archaic Techniques of Ecstasy*, trans. Willard Trask (New York: Bollingen Series LXXVI), pp. 210-12, being a summary of Uno Harva, *Die religiösen Vorstellungen der altaischen Völker* (Helsinki, 1938), pp. 334-45

See also nos. 204, 205, 208, 209

174. THE WINNEBAGO INDIAN ROAD TO THE LAND OF THE DEAD

Before the spirit of the departed starts his journey to the nether world, he is carefully informed of the surprises and dangers of the voyage and is duly instructed how to overcome them.

I suppose you are not far away, that indeed you are right behind me. Here is the tobacco and here is the pipe which you must keep in front of you as you go along. Here also are the fire and the food which your relatives have prepared for your journey.

In the morning when the sun rises you are to start. You will not have gone very far before you come to a wide road. That is the road you must take. As you go along you will notice something on your road. Take your war club and strike it and throw it behind you. Then go on without looking back. As you go farther you will again come across some obstacle. Strike it and throw it behind you and do not look back. Farther on you will come across some animals, and these also you must strike and throw behind you. Then go on and do not look back. The objects you throw behind you will come to those relatives whom you have left behind you on earth. They will represent victory in war, riches, and animals for food.

When you have gone but a short distance from the last place where you threw the objects behind, you will come to a round lodge and there you will find an old woman. She is the one who is to give you further information. She will ask you, 'Grandson, what is your name?' This you must tell her. Then you must say, 'Grandmother, when I was about to start from the earth I was given the following objects with which I was to act as mediator between you and the human beings [i.e., the pipe, tobacco, and food].' Then you must put the stem of the pipe in the old woman's mouth and say, 'Grandmother, I have made all my relatives lonesome, my parents, my brothers, and all the others. I would therefore like to have them obtain victory in war, and honours. That was my desire as I left them downhearted upon the earth. I would that they could have all that life which I left behind me on earth. This is what they asked. This, likewise, they asked me, that they should not have to travel on this road for some time to come. They also asked to be blessed with those things that people are accustomed to have on earth. All this they wanted me to ask of you when I started from the earth. They told me to follow the four steps that would be imprinted with blue marks, grandmother.' 'Well, grandson, you are young but you are wise. It is good. I will now boil some food for you.'

Thus she will speak to you and then put a kettle on the fire and boil some rice for you. If you eat it you will have a headache. Then she will say, 'Grandson, you have a headache, let me cup it for you.' Then she will break open your skull and take out your brains and you will forget all about your people on earth and where you came from. You will not worry about your relatives. You will become like a holy spirit. Your thoughts will not go as far as the earth, as there will be nothing carnal about you.

Now the rice that the old woman will boil will really be lice. For that reason you will be finished with everything evil. Then you will go on stepping in the four footsteps mentioned before and that were imprinted with blue earth. You are to take the four steps because the road will fork there. All your relatives who died before you will be there. As you journey on you will come to a fire running across the earth from one end to the other. There will be a bridge across it but it will be difficult to cross because it is continually swinging. However, you will be able to cross it safely, for you have all the guides about whom the warriors spoke to you. They will take you over and take care of you.

Well, we have told you a good road to take. If anyone tells a falsehood in speaking of the spirit-road, you will fall off the bridge and be burned. However you need not worry for you will pass over safely. As you proceed from that place the spirits will come to meet you and take you to the village where the chief lives. There you will give him the tobacco and ask for those objects of which we spoke to you, the same you asked of the old woman. There you will meet all the relatives that died before you. They will be living in a large lodge. This you must enter.

Paul Radin, *The Winnebago Tribe*, in Thirty-eighth Annual Report, Bureau of American Ethnology (Washington, D.C., 1923), pp. 143-4

175. THE ROAD TO THE SOUL'S WORLD, AS CONCEIVED BY THE THOMPSON RIVER TRIBES (BRITISH COLUMBIA)

The country of the souls is underneath us, toward the sunset; the trail leads through a dim twilight. Tracks of the people who last went over it. and of their dogs, are visible. The path winds along until it meets another road which is a short cut used by the shamans when trying to intercept a departed soul. The trail now becomes much straighter and smoother, and is painted red with ochre. After a while it winds to the westward, descends a long gentle slope, and terminates at a wide shallow stream of very clear water. This is spanned by a long slender log, on which the tracks of the souls may be seen. After crossing, the traveller finds himself again on the trail, which now ascends to a height heaped with an immense pile of clothes—the belongings which the souls have brought from the land of the living and which they must leave here. From this point the trail is level, and gradually grows lighter. Three guardians are stationed along this road, one on either side of the river and the third at the end of the path; it is their duty to send back those souls whose time is not yet come to enter the land of the dead. Some souls pass the first two of these, only to be turned back by the third, who is their chief and is an orator who sometimes sends messages to the living by the returning souls. All of these men are very old, grey-headed, wise, and venerable. At the end of the trail is a great lodge, mound-like in form, with doors at the eastern and the western sides, and with a double row of fires extending through it. When the deceased friends of a person expect his soul to arrive, they assemble here and talk about his death. As the deceased reaches the entrance, he hears people on the other side talking, laughing, singing, and beating drums. Some stand at the door to welcome him and call his name. On entering, a wide country of diversified aspect spreads out before him. There is a sweet smell of flowers and an abundance of grass, and all around are berry-bushes laden with ripe fruit. The air is pleasant and still, and it is always light and warm. More than half the people are dancing and singing to the accompaniment of drums. All are naked but do not seem to notice it. The people are delighted to see the new comer, take him up on their shoulders, run around with him, and make a great noise.

H. B. Alexander, *North American Mythology* (Boston, 1916), pp. 147-9; adapted from James Teit, *Traditions of the Thompson River Indians of British Columbia* (Boston and New York, 1898)

176. JOURNEY TO THE LAND OF THE GRANDFATHER:
A GUARAYÚ BELIEF (EASTERN BOLIVIA)

Soon after burial the liberated soul of the deceased started on a long and dangerous journey to the land of the mythical ancestor, Tamoi, or Grandfather, who lived somewhere in the west. It had to choose first between two paths. One was wide and easy. The other was narrow and obstructed with weeds and tobacco plants, but it followed this if it was wide and courageous. Soon the soul came to a large river which it had to cross on the back of a ferocious alligator. The alligator ferried the soul over only if it knew how to accompany the alligator's chant by rhythmically stamping its bamboo tube. It then came to another river which it could pass only by jumping on a tree trunk that floated at great speed to and fro between the two banks. If the soul fell, palometa fish would tear it to pieces. Shortly after this it neared the abode of Izoi-tamoi, Grandfather of Worms, who looked enormous from a distance but became smaller and smaller as he was approached. If the deceased had been a bad man, however, the process was reversed; the Grandfather of Worms grew to gigantic proportions and cleaved the sinner in two. Next, the soul had to travel through a dark region where it lit its way by burning a bunch of straw which relatives had put in the grave. However, it had to carry its torch behind its back lest the light be put out by huge bats. When the soul arrived near a beautiful ceiba tree full of humming birds, it washed itself in a brook and shot a few of these birds, without hurting them, and plucked their feathers for Tamoi's headdress. Then the soul kicked the ceiba trunk to notify its relatives that it had reached that place. The next obstacle was the Itacaru, two rocks which clashed and recoiled on its path. The stones allowed the soul a short interval to pass through if it knew how to address them.

At a crossroad the soul was examined by a gallinazo bird, who made sure that, like all good Guarayú, it had perforated lips and ears. If it did not possess these mutilations, it was misled by the bird. Two further ordeals awaited the journeying soul; it had to endure being tickled by a monkey without laughing, and to walk past a magic tree without listening to the voices which issued from it and without even looking at it. The tree was endowed with complete knowledge of the soul's past life. To resist these temptations, the soul pounded its stamping tube on the ground. A further danger took the form of coloured grasses which blinded the soul and caused it to lose its way. Finally the soul arrived at a large avenue lined with blossoming trees full of harmonious birds and knew then that it had reached the land of the Grandfather. It announced its arrival by stamping the ground with its bamboo tube. The Grandfather welcomed the soul with friendly words and washed it with a magic water which restored its youth and good looks. From then on, the soul lived happily, drinking chicha and carrying on the routine activities of its former life.

Alfred Métraux, *The Native Tribes of Eastern Bolivia and Western Matto Grosso*, Bureau of American Ethnology, Bulletin 134 (Washington, D.C., 1942), pp. 105-6

177. A POLYNESIAN JOURNEY INTO THE NETHER WORLD

This story . . . was told to Mr. Shortland [Edward Shortland, on whose account this summary is based] by a servant of his named Te Wharewera. An aunt of this man died in a solitary hut near the banks of Lake Rotorua. Being a lady of rank she was left in her hut, the door and windows were made fast, and the dwelling was abandoned, as her death had made it tapu. But a day of two after, Te Wharewera with some others paddling in a canoe near the place at early morning saw a figure on the shore beckoning to them. It was the aunt come to life again, but weak and cold and famished. When sufficiently restored by their timely help, she told her story. Leaving her body, her spirit had taken the flight toward the North Cape, and arrived at the entrance of Reigna. There, holding on by the stem of the creeping akeake-plant, she descended the precipice, and found herself on the sandy beach of a river. Looking around, she espied in the distance an enormous bird, taller than a man, coming towards her with rapid strides. This terrible object so frightened her, that her first thought was to try to return up the steep cliff; but seeing an old man paddling a small canoe towards her she ran to meet him, and so escaped the bird. When she had been safely ferried across she asked the old Charon, mentioning the name of her family, where the spirits of her kindred dwelt. Following the path the old man pointed out, she was surprised to find it just such a path as she had been used to on earth; the aspect of the country, the trees, shrubs, and plants were all familiar to her. She reached the village and among the crowd assembled there she found her father and many near relations; they saluted her, and welcomed her with the wailing chant which Maoris always address to people met after long absence. But when her father had asked about his living relatives, and especially about her own child, he told her she must go back to earth, for no one was left to take care of his grandchild. By his orders she refused to touch the food that the dead people offered her, and in spite of their efforts to detain her, her father got her safely into the canoe, crossed with her, and parting gave her from under his cloak two enormous sweet potatoes to plant at home for his grandchild's especial eating. But as she began to climb the precipice again, two pursuing infant spirits pulled her back, and she only escaped by flinging the roots at them, which they stopped to eat, while she scaled the rock by help of the akeake-stem, till she reached the earth and flew back to where she had left her body. On returning to life she found herself in darkness, and what had passed seemed as a dream, till she perceived that she was deserted and the door fast, and concluded that she had really died and come to life again. When morning dawned, a faint light entered by the crevices of the shut-up house, and she saw on the floor near her a calabash partly full of red ochre mixed with water; this she eagerly drained to the dregs, and then feeling a little stronger, succeeded in opening the door and crawling down to the beach, where her friends soon after found her. Those who listened to her tale firmly believed the reality of her adventures, but it was much regretted that she had not brought back at least one of the huge sweet-potatoes, as evidence of her visit to the land of spirits.

Sir Edward Burnett Tylor, *Religion in Primitive Culture* (New York: Harper Torchbook, 1958), pp. 136-8; summarizing Edward Shortland, *Traditions and Superstitions of the New Zealanders* (London, 1854), pp. 150 ff. Tylor's book first published as *Primitive Culture*

F. GREEK AND ROMAN CONCEPTIONS OF DEATH AND IMMORTALITY

178. 'EVEN IN THE HOUSE OF HADES THERE IS LEFT SOMETHING . . .'

(Homer, 'Iliad,' XXIII, 61-81, 99-108)

The ghost of Patroklos appears to Achilleus.

And at that time sleep caught him and was drifted sweetly about him, washing
the sorrows out of his mind, for his shining limbs were grown weary
indeed, from running in chase of Hektor toward windy Ilion;
and there appeared to him the ghost of unhappy Patroklos
all in his likeness for stature, and the lovely eyes, and voice,
and wore such clothing as Patroklos had worn on his body.
The ghost came and stood over his head and spoke a word to him:
'You sleep, Achilleus; you have forgotten me; but you were not
careless of me when I lived, but only in death. Bury me
as quickly as may be, let me pass through the gates of Hades.
The souls, the images of dead men, hold me at a distance,
and will not let me cross the river and mingle among them,
but I wander as I am by Hades' house of the wide gates.
And I call upon you in sorrow, give me your hand; no longer
shall I come back from death, once you give me my rite of burning.
No longer shall you and I, alive, sit apart from our other
beloved companions to make our plans, since the bitter destiny
that was given me when I was born has opened its jaws to take me.
And you, Achilleus like the gods, have your own destiny;
to be killed under the wall of the prospering Trojans. . . .
So he spoke, and with his own arms reached for him, but could not
take him, but the spirit went underground, like vapour,
with a thin cry, and Achilleus started awake, staring,
and drove his hands together, and spoke, and his words were sorrowful:
'Oh, wonder! Even in the house of Hades there is left something,
a soul and an image, but there is no real heart of life in it.

53

For all night long the phantom of unhappy Patroklos
stood over me in lamentation and mourning, and the likeness
to him was wonderful, and it told me each thing I should do.'

Translation by Richmond Lattimore. Homer's *Iliad*
(Chicago: University of Chicago Press, 1951), pp. 136-7

179. THE MEAD OF ASPHODEL, WHERE THE SPIRITS DWELL . . .': THE HOMERIC OTHER WORLD

(Homer, 'Odyssey,' XXIV, 1-18)

Meanwhile Cyllenian Hermes called forth the spirits of the wooers.
He held in his hands his wand, a fair wand of gold, wherewith he lulls
to sleep the eyes of whom he will, while others again he wakens even
out of slumber; with this he roused and led the spirits, and they followed gibbering. And as in the innermost recess of a wondrous cave
bats flit about gibbering, when one has fallen from off the rock from
the chain in which they cling to one another, so these went with him
gibbering, and Hermes, the Helper, led them down the dank ways.
Past the streams of Oceanus they went, past the rock Leucus, past the
gates of the sun and the land of dreams, and quickly came to the
mead of the asphodel, where the spirits dwell, phantoms of men who
have done with toils. Here they found the spirit of Achilles, son of
Peleus, and those of Patroclus, of peerless Antilochus, and of Aias,
who in comeliness and form was the goodliest of all the Danaans after
the peerless son of Peleus.

Translation by A. T. Murray in the Loeb Classical
Library, vol. II (New York, 1919), p. 403

180. A ROMAN VIEW OF THE AFTER LIFE: THE DREAM OF SCIPIO

(Cicero, 'On the Republic,' VI, 14-26)

'The Dream of Scipio' is the conclusion of Cicero's treatise On the
Republic, probably written in 54 B.C. The dialogue is assumed to have
taken place during the Latin holidays in 129 B.C., in the garden of
Scipio Africanus the Younger. Scipio relates a dream in which he saw

his grandfather, Scipio Africanus the Elder. 'When I recognized him, I trembled with terror, but he said: "Courage, Scipio, do not be afraid, but remember carefully what I am to tell you." '

(14) By this time I was thoroughly terrified, not so much fearing death as the treachery of my own kind. Nevertheless, I [went on and] inquired of Africanus whether he himself was still alive, and also whether my father Paulus was, and also the others whom we think of as having ceased to be.

'Of course they are alive,' he replied. 'They have taken their flight from the bonds of the body as from a prison. Your so-called life [on earth] is really death. Do you not see your father Paulus coming to meet you?'

At the sight of my father I broke down and cried. But he embraced me and kissed me and told me not to weep. (15) As soon as I had controlled my grief and could speak, I began: 'Why, O best and saintliest of fathers, since here [only] is life worthy of the name, as I have just heard from Africanus, why must I live a dying life on earth? Why may I not hasten to join you here?'

'No indeed,' he replied. 'Unless that God whose temple is the whole visible universe releases you from the prison of the body, you cannot gain entrance here. For men were given life for the purpose of culti-vating that globe, called Earth, which you see at the centre of this temple. Each has been given a soul, [a spark] from these eternal fires which you call stars and planets, which are globular and rotund and are animated by divine intelligence, and which with marvellous velocity revolve in their established orbits. Like all god-fearing men, therefore, Publius, you must leave the soul in the custody of the body, and must not quit the life on Earth unless you are summoned by the one who gave it to you; otherwise you will be seen to shirk the duty assigned by God to man.

(16) 'But Scipio, like your grandfather here, like myself, who was your father, cultivate justice and the sense of duty [pietas], which are of great importance in relation to parents and kindred but even more in relation to one's country. Such a life [spent in the service of one's country] is a highway to the skies, to the fellowship of those who have completed their earthly lives and have been released from the body and now dwell in that place which you see yonder' (it was the circle of dazzling brilliance which blazed among the stars), 'which you, using a term borrowed from the Greeks, call the Milky Way.'

Looking about from this high vantage point, everything appeared to me to be marvellous and beautiful. There were stars which we never see from the Earth, and the dimensions of all of them were greater than we have ever suspected. The smallest among them was the one which, being farthest from Heaven and nearest the Earth, shone with a borrowed light [the Moon]. The size of the stars. however, far exceeded that of the Earth. Indeed, the later seemed so small that I was humiliated with our empire, which is only a point where we touch the surface of the globe. . . .

(18) When I had recovered from my astonishment over this great panorama, and had come to myself, I asked: 'Tell me what is this loud, sweet harmony that fills my ears?'

He replied, 'This music is produced by the impulse and motion of these spheres themselves. The unequal intervals between them are arranged according to a strict proportion, and so the high notes blend agreeably with the low, and thus various sweet harmonies are produced. Such immense revolutions cannot, of course, be so swiftly carried out in silence, and it is only natural that one extreme should produce deep tones and the other high ones. Accordingly, this highest sphere of Heaven, which bears the stars, and whose revolution is swifter, produces a high shrill sound, whereas the lowest sphere, that of the Moon, rotates with the deepest sound. The Earth, of course, the ninth sphere, remains fixed and immovable in the centre of the universe. But the other eight spheres, two of which move with the same speed, produce seven different sounds—a number, by the way, which is the key to almost everything. Skilful men reproducing this celestial music on stringed instruments have thus opened the way for their own return to this heavenly region, as other men of outstanding genius have done by spending their lives on Earth in the study of things divine. . . .'

(26) 'Yes, you must use you best efforts,' he replied, 'and be sure that it is not you who are mortal, but only your body; nor is it you whom your outward form represents. Your spirit is your true self, not that bodily form that can be pointed out with the finger. Know yourself, therefore, to be a god—if indeed a god is a being that lives, feels, remembers, and foresees, that rules, governs, and moves the body over which it is set, just as the supreme God above us rules this world. And just as that eternal God moves the universe, which is partly mortal, so an eternal spirit moves the fragile body. . . .

Translation by Frederick C. Grant, in his *Ancient Roman Religion*, Library of Religion paperbook series (New York, 1957), pp. 147-56

181. EMPEDOCLES ON THE TRANSMIGRATION OF THE SOUL

('Fragments' 115, 117, 118)

There is an oracle of Necessity, ancient decree of the gods, eternal and sealed with broad oaths: whenever one of those demi-gods, whose lot is long-lasting life, has sinfully defiled his dear limbs with bloodshed, or following strife has sworn a false oath, thrice ten thousand seasons does he wander far from the blessed, being born throughout that time in the forms of all manner of mortal things and changing one baleful path of life for another. The might of the air pursues him into the sea, the sea spews him forth on to the dry land, the earth casts him into the rays of the burning sun, and the sun into the eddies of air. One takes him from the other, but all alike abhor him. Of these I too am now one, a fugitive from the gods and a wanderer, who put my trust in raving strife. (*Frag.* 115)

I wept and wailed when I saw the unfamiliar place. (*Frag.* 118)

For already have I once been a boy and a girl, a fish and a bird and a dumb sea fish. (*Frag.* 117)

> Empedocles texts in G. S. Kirk and J. E. Raven, translators, *The Presocratic Philosophers* (Cambridge, Eng., 1957)

182. PLATO ON TRANSMIGRATION: THE MYTH OF ER

('Republic,' x, 614 b)

It is not, let me tell you, said I, the tale to Alcinous told that I shall unfold, but the tale of a warrior bold, Er, the son of Armenius, by race a Pamphylian. He once upon a time was slain in battle, and when the corpses were taken up on the tenth day already decayed, was found intact, and having been brought home, at the moment of his funeral, on the twelfth day as he lay upon the pyre, revived, and after coming to life related what, he said, he had seen in the world beyond. He said that when his soul went forth from his body he journeyed with a great company and that they came to a mysterious region where there were two openings side by side in the earth, and above and over against them in the heaven two others, and that judges were sitting between these, and that after every judgement they bade the righteous journey to the right and upward through the heaven with tokens attached to them in front of the judgement passed upon them, and the unjust to take the road to the left and downward, they too wearing behind signs of all that had befallen them, and that when he himself drew near they told him that he must be the messenger to mankind to tell them of that other world, and they charged him to give ear and to observe everything in the place. And so he said that here he saw, by each opening of heaven and earth, the souls departing after judgement had been passed upon them, while, by the other pair of openings, there came up from the one in the earth souls full of squalor and dust, and from the second there came down from heaven a second procession of souls clean and pure, and that those which arrived from time to time appeared to have come as it were from a long journey and gladly departed to the meadow and encamped there as at a festival, and acquaintances greeted one another, and those which came from the earth questioned the others about conditions up yonder, and those from heaven asked how it fared with those others. And they told their stories to one another, the one lamenting and wailing as they recalled how many and how dreadful things they had suffered and seen in their journey beneath the earth—it lasted a thousand years—while those from heaven related their delights and visions of a beauty beyond words. To tell it all, Glaucon, would take all our time, but the sum, he said, was this. For all the wrongs they had ever done to anyone and all whom they had severally wronged they had paid the penalty in turn tenfold each, and the measure of this was by periods of a hundred years each, so that on the assumption that this was the length of human life the punishment might be ten times the crime—as for example that if anyone had been the cause of many deaths or had betrayed cities and armies and reduced them to slavery, or had been participant in any other iniquity, they might receive in requital pains tenfold for each of these wrongs, and again if any had done deeds of kindness and had been just and holy men they might receive their due reward in the same measure. And other things not worthy of record he said of those who had just been born and lived but a short time, and he had still greater requitals to tell of piety and impiety towards the gods and parents and of self-slaughter.

Translation by Paul Shorey, in Hamilton and Cairns (eds.), *Plato: The Collected Dialogues* (New York: Bollingen Series LXXI, 1961), pp. 838-40

183. PLATO ON THE IMMORTALITY OF THE SOUL

('Meno,' 81 b)

MENO: What was it, and who were they?

SOCRATES: Those who tell it are priests and priestesses of the sort who make it their business to be able to account for the functions which they perform. Pindar speaks of it too, and many another of the poets who are divinely inspired. What they say is this—see whether you think they are speaking the truth. They say that the soul of man is immortal. At one time it comes to an end—that which is called death—and at another is born again, but is never finally exterminated. On these grounds a man must live all his days as righteously as possible. For those from whom

> *Persephone receives requital for ancient doom,*
> *In the ninth year she restores again*
> *Their souls to the sun above.*
> *From whom rise noble kings*
> *And the swift in strength and greatest in wisdom,*
> *And for the rest of time*
> *They are called heroes and sanctified by men.*[1]

Thus the soul, since it is immortal and has been born many times, and has seen all things both here and in the other world, has learned everything that is.

Note

1 Pindar, *Fragment* 133.

Translated by W. K. C. Guthrie, in Hamilton and Cairns (eds.), Plato: *The Collected Dialogues* (New York: Bollingen Series LXXI, 1961), p. 364

See also nos. 149, 159

G. ORPHEUS MYTHS

184. A POLYNESIAN ORPHEUS

A Maori hero, Hutu, went down to the underworld in search of the soul of the princess, Pare, who had committed suicide after being humiliated by him. This story is reminiscent of Orpheus' descent to Hades to bring back the soul of his wife, Eurydice.

Once, when the lance which he had thrown, led Hutu to Pare's door, the young noble-woman, whose heart had been won by the youth's skill and presence, revealed to him her admiration and love and invited him to enter her house. But he refused her and departed. Overwhelmed with shame, she 'ordered her attendants to arrange everything in the house and put it in order. When this was done she sat alone and wept, and rose and hung herself.' Hutu, remorseful, fearful of the people's anger, determined to save her soul in the world below. First he sat down and chanted the priestly incantations having to do with death and the abode of the dead; then he rose and proceeded on his journey. He met Hine-nui-te-po (Great-lady-of-the-night), who presides over the Land of Shades. Ill-humoured as usual, when Hutu asked the way, she pointed out the path taken by the spirits of dogs to the lower regions; but her favour was eventually won by the presentation of the seeker's precious greenstone hand club. Mollified by the gift, the goddess pointed out the true route, cooked some fern root for him and put it into a basket, at the same time admonishing him to eat sparingly of it, for it must suffice him throughout the journey. Should he eat the food of the lower world, it would mean that, instead of his being able to bring back the spirit of Pare to the world of light, his own soul would be condemned to remain forever in the lower regions. The goddess advised him further, 'When you fly from this world, bow your head as you descend to the dark world; but when you are near the world below a wind from beneath will blow on you, and will raise your head up again, and you will be in a right position to alight on your feet. . . .' Hutu arrived safely in the world below, and on inquiring the whereabouts of Pare, was told that she was 'in the village.' Although the girl knew that Hutu had come and was seeking her, her shame led her to conceal herself. In the hope of luring her from her house, he organized contests in top spinning and javelin throwing, games which he knew she loved to watch. But never did she appear. At last Hutu, sore at heart, said to the others, 'Bring a very long tree and let us cut the branches off it.' This done, ropes were plaited and tied to the top, and the crown of the tree was bent down to the earth by the people's tugging at the ropes. Hutu climbed into the top, and another man sat on his back. Then Hutu shouted, 'Let go.' And the tree flung the young adventurer and his companion high into the air. Delighted at this exhibition, all the people shouted with glee. This was too much for Pare and she came to watch the new game. Finally she said, 'Let me also swing, but let me sit on your shoulders.'

Exuberant, Hutu answered, 'Keep hold of my neck, O Pare!' The top of the tree being again drawn down, it was released on the signal and flew skyward with such a rush as to fling the ropes against the under side of the upper world where they became entangled in the grass at the entrance to the realm of the shades. Climbing up the ropes with Pare on his back, Hutu emerged into the world of light. He went straightway to the settlement where the dead body of Pare was lying, and the spirit of the young chiefess reentered her body and it became alive.

> John White, *The Ancient History of the Maori*
> (Wellington, 1887-90), vol. II, pp. 164-7, as condensed
> by E. S. Craighill Handy, *Polynesian Religion*, Bernice
> P. Bishop Museum Bulletin 34 (Honolulu, 1927), pp. 81
> *ff.* (Cf. M. Eliade, *Shamanism: Archaic Techniques of
> Ecstasy*, trans. Willard Trask [New York, 1964],
> p. 368)

185. A CALIFORNIAN ORPHEUS: A TACHI YOKUT MYTH

The Orpheus myth is also popular among North American Indian tribes, especially in the western and eastern parts of the continent.

A Tachi had a fine wife who died and was buried. Her husband went to her grave and dug a hole near it. There he stayed watching, not eating, using only tobacco. After two nights he saw that she came up, brushed the earth off herself, and started to go to the island of the dead. The man tried to seize her but could not hold her. She went southeast and he followed her. Whenever he tried to hold her she escaped. He kept trying to seize her, however, and delayed her. At daybreak she stopped. He stayed there, but could not see her. When it began to be dark the woman got up again and went on. She turned westward and crossed Tulare Lake (or its inlet). At daybreak the man again tried to seize her but could not hold her. She stayed in the place during the day. The man remained in the same place, but again he could not see her. There was a good trail there, and he could see the footprints of his dead friend and relatives. In the evening his wife got up again and went on. They came to a river which flows westward towards San Luis Obispo, the river of the Tulamni (the description fits the Santa Maria, but the Tulamni are in the Tulare drainage, on and about Buena Vista lake). There the man caught up with his wife and there they stayed all day. He still had nothing to eat. In the evening she went on again, now northward. Then somewhere to the west of the Tachi country he caught up with her once more and they spent the day there. In the evening the woman got up and they went on northward, across the San Joaquin river, to the north or east of it. Again he overtook his wife. Then she said: 'What are you going to do? I am nothing now. How can you get my body back? Do you think you shall be able to do it?' He said: 'I think so.' She said: 'I think not. I am going to a different kind of a place now.' From daybreak on that man stayed there. In the evening the woman started once more and went down along the river; but he overtook her again. She did not talk to him. Then they stayed all day, and at night went on again. Now they were close to the island of the dead. It was joined to the land by a rising and falling bridge called *ch'eleli*. Under this bridge a river ran swiftly. The dead passed over this. When they were on the bridge, a bird suddenly fluttered up beside them and frightened them. Many fell off into the river, where they turned into fish. Now the chief of the dead said: 'Somebody has come.' They told him: 'There are two. One of them is alive; he stinks.' The chief said: 'Do not let him cross.' When the woman came on the island, he asked her: 'You have a companion?' and she told him: 'Yes, my husband.' He asked her: 'Is he coming here?' She said, 'I do not know. He is alive.' They asked the man: 'Do you want to come to this country?' He said: 'Yes.' Then they told him: 'Wait, I will see the chief.' They told the chief: 'He says that he wants to come to this country. We think he does not tell the truth.' 'Well, let him come across.' Now they intended to frighten him off the bridge. They said: 'Come on. The chief says you can cross.' Then the bird (*kacha*) flew up and tried to scare him, but did not make him fall off the bridge into the water. So they brought him before the chief. The chief said: 'This is a bad country. You should not have come. We have only your wife's soul *(ilit)*. She has left her bones with her body. I do not think we can give her back to you.' In the evening they danced. It was a round dance and they shouted. The chief said to the man: 'Look at your wife in the middle of the crowd. Tomorrow you will see no one.' Now the man stayed there three days. Then the chief said to some of the people: 'Bring that woman. Her husband wants to talk to her.' They brought the woman to him. He asked her: 'Is this your husband?' She said: 'Yes.' He asked her: 'Do you think you will go back to him?' She said: 'I do not think so. What do you wish?' The chief said: 'I think not. You must stay here. You cannot go back. You are worthless now.' Then he said to the man: 'Do you want to sleep with your wife?' He said: 'Yes, for a while. I want to sleep with her and talk to her.' Then he was allowed to sleep with her that night and they talked together. At daybreak the woman was vanished and he was sleeping next to a fallen oak. The chief said to him: 'Get up. It is late.' He opened his eyes and saw an oak instead of his wife. The chief said: 'You see that we cannot make your wife as she was. She is no good now. It is best that you go back. You have a good country there.' But the man said: 'No, I will stay.' The chief told him: 'No, do not. Come back here whenever you like, but go back now.' Nevertheless he man stayed there six days. Then he said: 'I am going back.' Then in the morning he started to go home. The chief told him: 'When you arrive, hide yourself. Then after six days emerge and make a dance.' Now the man returned. He told his parents: 'Make me a small house. In six days I will come out and dance.' Now he stayed there five days. Then his friends began to know that he had come back. 'Our relative has come back,' they all said. Now the man was in too much of a hurry. After five days he went out. In the evening he began to dance and danced all night, telling what he saw. In the morning when he had stopped dancing, he went to bathe. Then a rattlesnake bit him. He died. So he went back to island. He is there now. It is through him that the people know it is there. Every two days the island becomes full. Then the chief gathers the people. 'You must swim,' he says. The people stop dancing and bathe. Then the bird frightens them, and some turn to fish, and some to ducks; only a few come out of the water again as people. In this way room is made when the island is too full. The name of the chief there is Kandjidji.

A. L. Kroeber, *Indian Myths of South Central Cali-fornia*, University of California Publications, *American Archaeology and Ethnology*, vol. IV, no. 4 (1906-7), pp. 216-18

H. PARADISES

('Sukhāvatīvyūha,' chapters 15-18)

15. This world Sukhāvatī, Ānanda, which is the world system of the Lord Amitābha, is rich and prosperous, comfortable, fertile, delightful and crowded with many Gods and men. And in this world system, Ānanda, there are no hells, no animals, no ghosts, no Asuras and none of the inauspicious places of rebirth. And in this our world no jewels make their appearance like those which exist in the world system Sukhāvatī.

16. And that world system Sukhāvatī, Ānanda, emits many fragrant odours, it is rich in a great variety of flowers and fruits, adorned with jewel trees, which are frequented by flocks of various birds with sweet voices, which the Tathāgata's miraculous power has conjured up. And these jewel trees, Ānanda, have various colours, many colours, many hundreds of thousands of colours. They are variously composed of the seven precious things, in varying combinations, i.e. of gold, silver, beryl, crystal, coral, red pearls or emerald. Such jewel trees, and clusters of banana trees and rows of palm trees, all made of precious things, grow everywhere in this Buddha-field. On all sides it is surrounded with golden nets, and all round covered with lotus flowers made of all the precious things. Some of the lotus flowers are half a mile in circumference, others up to ten miles. And from each jewel lotus issue thirty-six hundred thousand kotis of rays. And at the end of each ray there issue thirty-six hundred thousand kotis of Buddhas, with golden-coloured bodies, who bear the thirty-two marks of the superman, and who, in all the ten directions, go into countless world systems, and there demonstrate Dharma.

17. And further, Ānanda, in this Buddha-field there are nowhere any mountains,—black mountains, jewel mountains, Sumerus, kings of mountains, circular mountains and great circular mountains. But the Buddha-field is everywhere even, delightful like the palm of the

hand, and in all its parts the ground contains a great variety of jewels and gems. . . .

18. And many kinds of rivers flow along in this world system Sukhāvatī. There are great rivers there, one mile broad, and up to fifty miles broad and twelve miles deep. And these rivers flow along calmly, their water is fragrant with manifold agreeable odours, in them are bunches of flowers to which various jewels adhere, and they resound with various sweet sounds. And the sound which issues from these great rivers is as pleasant as that of a musical instrument, which consists of hundreds of thousands of kotis of parts, and which, skilfully played, emits a heavenly music. It is deep, commanding, distinct, clear, pleasant to the ear, touching the heart, delightful, sweet, pleasant, and one never tires of hearing it, it always agrees with one and one likes to hear it, like the words 'Impermanent, peaceful, calm, and not-self.' Such is the sound that reaches the ears of those beings.

And, Ānanda, both the banks of those great rivers are lined with variously scented jewel trees, and from them bunches of flowers, leaves and branches of all kinds hang down. And if those beings wish to indulge in sports full of heavenly delights on those river-banks, then, after they have stepped into the water, the water in each case rises as high as they wish it to,—up to the ankles, or the knees, or the hips, or their sides, or their ears. And heavenly delights arise. Again, if beings wish the water to be cold, for them it becomes cold; if they wish it to be hot, for them it becomes hot; if they wish it to be hot and cold, for them it becomes hot and cold, to suit their pleasure. And those rivers flow along, full of water scented with the finest odours, and covered with beautiful flowers, resounding with the sounds of many birds, easy to ford, free from mud, and with golden sand at the bottom. And all the wishes those beings may think of, they all will be fulfilled, as long as they are rightful.

And as to the pleasant sound which issues from the water (of those rivers), that reaches all the parts of this Buddha-field. And everyone hears the pleasant sound he wishes to hear, i.e. he hears of the Buddha, the Dharma, the Samgha, of the (six) perfections, the (ten) stages, the powers, the grounds of self-confidence, of the special dharmas of a Buddha, of the analytical knowledge, of emptiness, the signless, and the wishless, of the uneffected, the unborn, of non-production, non-existence, non-cessation, of calm, quietude and peace, of the great friendliness, the great compassion, the great sympathetic joy, the great evenmindedness, of the patient acceptance of things which fail to be produced, and of the acquisition of the stage where one is consecrated (as a Tathāgata). And, hearing this, one gains the exalted zest and joyfulness, which is associated with detachment, dispassion, calm, cessation, Dharma, and brings about the state of mind which leads to the accomplishment of enlightenment. And nowhere in this world-system Sukhāvatī does one hear of anything unwholesome, nowhere of the hindrances, nowhere of the states of punishment, the states of woe and the bad destinies, nowhere of suffering. Even of feelings which are neither pleasant nor unpleasant one does not hear here, how much less of suffering! And that, Ānanda, is the reason why this world-system is called the 'Happy Land' (Sukhāvatī). But all this describes it only in brief, not in detail. One aeon might well reach its end while one proclaims the reasons for happiness in the world-system Sukhāvatī, and still one could not come to the end of (the enumeration of) the reasons for happiness.

Sukhāvatīvyūha, ch. 15-17, 18. Translation by Edward Conze, in Conze *et al.*, *Buddhist Texts through the Ages* (Oxford: Bruno Cassirer (Publishers) Ltd., 1954).

187. THE VISION OF ALLAH IN THE OTHER WORLD

Said Hammad b. Sulaiman: When the blessed have entered Paradise and have established themselves there in pleasure and delight, in a magnificent kingdom, a noble residence where they are in security and tranquility, they quite forget there what they were promised in this world of how they would [one day] see Allah and go to visit Him, so occupied are they with the blessings and the pleasures they are enjoying there. So while they are thus, behold, an angel from before Allah—mighty and majestic is He—looks down upon them from one of the mighty walls of Paradise, from an eminence so high that not a thing in Paradise is hidden from him. [It is a wall] made of glistening pearl whose light shines over against the Throne and shines to the highest point of heaven. This angel will call out at the top of his voice: 'O people of Paradise, greeting of peace to you,' yet with a voice so full of compassion that, though it is so loud, all ears incline to it and all faces turn toward it, all souls being moved by it, rejoicing at it, and responding eagerly to it. All of them hear the voice and take cognizance that this is a herald from before Allah—mighty and majestic is He. It will evoke no doubt in them, so they will respond:

'Labbaika! Labbaika!¹ O summoner from Allah, our Lord. We have heard and we respond.' Then he will say: 'Welcome to you, O ye saints of Allah! Welcome! most Welcome! Allah—mighty and majestic is He—sends you greeting of peace, saying that He is well pleased with you [and asking] are ye well pleased with Him.' They will reply: 'Praise be to Allah who has guided us to this, for we were not such as would have been guided had not Allah guided us (VII, 43/41). Praise be to Him, since He is well pleased with us and has made us well satisfied. To Him be praise and thanksgiving, since He has been bountiful to us and given us [all this].' Then (the angel) will say: 'O saints of Allah, Allah—glory be to Him—sends you greeting of peace and says: "Have I fulfilled the promises I made to you in the world, or have I come short of them in any way?"' They will answer: 'Praise be to Allah, His are the gifts and the favours. He has indeed fulfilled His promises and bestowed on us bounty from Himself, this Paradise, in which we go about wherever we wish.' Then [the angel] will say to them: 'Allah—glory be to Him—gives you greeting of peace, and reminds you that in the world He promised you that in Paradise you would visit Him, approach Him, and look upon Him. Now He would fulfil what He promised you, so He gives you here and now permission to prepare yourselves to have your happiness made complete in His presence.'

When they hear that, everything they have been enjoying there and all they have so far attained in Paradise will seem to them a little thing compared with that exceeding great happiness. Indeed, all that Paradise contains will seem insignificant over against the fact that Allah is well pleased with them and [is allowing them] to visit Him and look upon Him. So they will get themselves ready for a visit to their Lord in their finest estate and their most beautiful attire. They will clothe themselves with the most precious robes and the most fragrant perfumes, and mount the finest of horses and the most nobly born steeds, the most precious that they have, and putting crowns upon their heads they will come forth, each man from his palace and his garden, till he reaches the farthest end of his property and moves out into the paths of Paradise, his *wildān*² preceding him and guiding him on the way to the visitation of the most illustrious King. Meanwhile they raise their voices in expressions of remembrance and encomium and hallelujahs (*tahlīl*), and whenever any man among them comes out into the paths of Paradise he meets his brother [Muslim] who has come out for the same purpose that he has.

Thus they will journey along till they come to a broad open space at the borders of Paradise, where the ground is unencumbered, vacant, white, and camphored, its soil being of camphor mixed with musk and ambergris, and its stones of pearl and jacinth. There they will assemble, preceded by the angel who had summoned them and who has travelled on ahead of them till he has brought them to this Garden of Eden. Allah will have given a call to this Garden, [saying]; 'Adorn yourself, for I have called My saints to visit Me within you,' so the Garden will have adorned itself with the most exquisite and beautiful adornment, and its attendants and *wildān* will likewise have got themselves ready. So when the saints arrive at the gate of the Garden, the angel will precede them, having with him the people of Paradise, and all of them will cry; 'Greeting to you, O ye angels of our Lord.' Then there will be opened for them a gate between whose leaves is the distance between the East and the West here on earth. This gate is of green emerald and over it are curtains of light of such brightness as almost to destroy the sight. They will enter and pour out into a valley-bed there whose enormous size, both in length and breadth, is known only to Him who created it by His power and fashioned it in His wisdom. Its soil is of finest musk and saffron and ambergris, its stones of jacinths and jewels, its little pebbles and rubble are of gold, while on its banks are trees whose limbs hang down, whose branches are low, whose fruits are within easy reach, whose birds sing sweetly, whose colours shine brightly, whose flowers blossom in splendour, and from which comes a breeze [so delightful] as to reduce to insignificance all other delights, one needle's-eye full of which, were it sent to this world, would cure all the sick.

Beneath these trees are chairs and benches of light that gleam, chairs and benches of jacinth and of jewels, and the like of red gold, of green emerald, of musk and ambergris, set there for the prophets, the messengers, then for the saints and the pious, then for the martyrs and the just, then for the Blessed from among all the rest of the people. Over [these seats] are cloths of brocade and satin and green silk, very precious, the silk woven and hemmed with jacinths and with jewels, and [on them] also are cushions of red brocade. On these they will be given permission to seat themselves in accordance with the honourable rank each has. They will be met by cries of welcome and applause, with ascriptions of honour and merit. So each man of them will take his station according to the measure of honour he has with his Lord, and his position of nearness to Him and in His favour, while the angels and the *wildān* show them great respect in seating them. Then, when every man has taken his place and settled himself, according to his rank, orders will be given that they be served with the finest food. So they will eat it and enjoy it with such pleasure that they forget any food that they have eaten hitherto, and everything they have ever known before seems insignificant to them. [It will be served to them] on platters the like of which they have never seen before and on tables whose like they have never beheld. Then orders will be given that they be served the finest kinds of fruit such as they never before have seen, and they will eat of these fruits and enjoy thereof as much as they desire. Then orders will be given that they be served the finest varieties of drinks such as they never yet have drunk, [served to them] in vessels of pearl and jacinth which shine brilliantly, giving out lights the like of whose splendour and loveliness they have hitherto never beheld. So they will drink and enjoy it, and then orders will be given for them to be [perfumed] with perfumes such as they have never before enjoyed. Then orders will be given for them to be clothed with garments [of honour] the like of which they have not seen even in Paradise, and of such splendour and beauty as they have never before had for their delight.

This will be their state, so ask not about their happiness and their joy there, for all that they have had before now seems to them of no account. Then Allah—glory be to Him—will say: 'O My saints, O My servants, have I fulfilled to you what I promised you in the world? Have I amply fulfilled My promise?' They will answer: 'Yea, O our Lord, by Thy might, Thou hast fulfilled to us Thy promise and hast amply fulfilled what thou didst promise us.' Then He—glory be to Him—will say: 'Nay, by My might, there still remains for you one thing which you covet yet more and which has a still higher place in your estimation. What is there after you have come to Me but that you should look upon Me, that thereby your blessedness may be complete?' Then He—glory be to Him—will give command to the veils of light so they will be raised, and to the dread awfulness so that it is set aside. Then He—glory be to Him—will reveal Himself as them and they will look upon Him. Thus will they see Him without suffering any injury or any harm, and no joy can equal their joy in that, nor can any happiness or delight stand beside their happiness in that. So they will fall down before their Lord in prostration and deep humility, saying: 'Glory be to Thee, O our Lord. In Thy praise Thou art blessed and exalted, and blessed is Thy name.'

Notes

1 This exclamation, whose meaning is little understood, was the ancient cry which used to be raised by those approaching the sacred shrine at Mecca. It is still used by Muslim pilgrims at the present day. The technical word for making devotional use of this exclamation is *talbiya*.

2 Each of the Blessed in Paradise has a provision of male and female attendants of celestial origin. The *wildān* are the celestial youths who wait on them and the *hūrīs* are the celestial damsels.

Translation and notes by Arthur Jeffery, *Islam: Muhammad and His Religion* (New York: Liberal Arts Press, 1958) pp. 98-103; trans. from Ibn Makhlūf, *Kitāb al'Ulūm al-fākhira fī'n-nazr fī Umūr al-Ākhira* (Cairo, 1317 A.H.=A.D. 1899), II, 151-3

I. THE END OF THE WORLD

188. AHURA MAZDA TEACHES YIMA HOW TO SAVE ALL THAT IS BEST AND FAIREST IN THE WORLD

('Vidēvdāt,' Fargard II)

A terrible winter is approaching, a winter which is to destroy every living creature. Yima, the first man and first king, is advised to build a well-defended enclosure (vara) in which he is to keep the finest representatives of every kind of animal and plant. They live for a life of perfect happiness there.

(46) And Ahura Mazda spake unto Yima, saying:

'O fair Yima, son of Vīvanghat! Upon the material world the evil winters are about to fall, that shall bring the fierce, deadly frost; upon the material world the evil winters are about to fall, that shall make snowflakes fall thick, even in *aredvī* deep on the highest tops of the mountains.

(52) 'And the beasts that live in the wilderness, and those that live on the tops of the mountains, and those that live in the bosom of the dale shall take shelter in underground abodes.

(57) 'Before that winter, the country would bear plenty of grass for cattle, before the waters had flooded it. Now after the melting of the snow, O Yima, a place wherein the footprint of a sheep may be seen will be a wonder in the world.

(61) 'Therefore make thee a Vara (enclosure), long as a riding-ground on every side of the square, and thither bring the seeds of sheep and oxen, of men, of dogs, of birds, and of red blazing fires.

Therefore make thee a Vara, long as a riding-ground on every side of the square, to be an abode for men; a Vara, long as a riding-ground on every side of the square, for oxen and sheep.

(65) 'There thou shalt make waters flow in a bed a *hathra* long; there thou shalt settle birds, on the green that never fades, with food that never fails. There thou shalt establish dwelling-places consisting of a house with a balcony, a courtyard, and a gallery.

(70) 'Thither thou shalt bring the seeds of men and women, of the greatest, best, and finest on this earth; thither thou shalt bring the seeds of every kind of cattle, of the greatest, best, and finest on this earth.

(74) 'Thither thou shalt bring the seeds of every kind of tree, of the highest of size and sweetest of odour on this earth; thither thou shalt bring the seeds of every kind of fruit, the best of savour and sweetest of odour. All those seeds shalt thou bring, two of every kind, to be kept inexhaustible there, so long as those men shall stay in the Vara.

(80) 'There shall be no humpbacked, none bulged forward there; no impotent, no lunatic; no one malicious, no liar; no one spiteful, none jealous; no one with decayed tooth, no leprous to be pent up, nor any of the brands wherewith Angra Mainyu stamps the bodies of mortals.

(87) 'In the largest part of the place thou shalt make nine streets, six in the middle part, three in the smallest. To the streets of the largest part thou shalt bring a thousand seeds of men and women; to the streets of the middle part, six hundred; to the streets of the smallest part, three hundred. That Vara thou shalt seal up with thy golden seal, and thou shalt make a door, and a window self-shining within.'

(93) Then Yima said within himself: 'How shall I manage to make that Vara which Ahura Mazda has commanded me to make?'

And Ahura Mazda said unto Yima: 'O fair Yima, son of Vīvanghat! Crush the earth with a stamp of thy heel, and then knead it with thy hands, as the potter does when kneading the potter's clay.'

Translation by James Darmesteter, *The Zend-Avesta*, part I, in *Sacred Books of the East*, IV (2nd ed.; Oxford 1895), pp. 15-18

189. THE BUDDHA FORETELLS THE GRADUAL DECLINE
OF RELIGION

('Anāgatavamsa')

Praise to that Lord, Arahant, perfect Buddha.
Thus have I heard: At one time the Lord was staying near Kapila-vatthu in the Banyan monastery on the bank of the river Rohani.

The End of the World

Then the venerable Sariputta questioned the Lord about the future Conqueror:

> 'The Hero that shall follow you,
> The Buddha—of what sort will he be?
> I want to hear of him in full.
> Let the Visioned One describe him.'

> When he had heard the Elder's speech
> The Lord spoke thus:
> 'I will tell you, Sariputta,
> Listen to my speech.

> 'In this auspicious aeon
> Three leaders have there been:
> Kakusandha, Konāgamana
> And the leader Kassapa too.

> 'I am now the perfect Buddha;
> And there will be Metteyya [i.e., Maitreya] too
> Before this same auspicious aeon
> Runs to the end of its years.

> 'The perfect Buddha, Metteyya
> By name, supreme of men.'

(Then follows a history of the previous existence of Metteyya . . . and then the description of the gradual decline of the religion:)

'How will it occur? After my decease there will first be five disappearances. What five? The disappearance of attainment (in the Dispensation), the disappearance of proper conduct, the disappearance of learning, the disappearance of the outward form, the disappearance of the relics. There will be these five disappearances.

'Here attainment means that for a thousand years only after the Lord's complete Nirvāna will monks be able to practise analytical insights. As time goes on and on these disciples of mine are non-returners and once-returners and stream-winners. There will be no disappearance of attainment for these. But with the extinction of the last stream-winner's life, attainment will have disappeared.

'This, Sariputta, is the disappearance of attainment.

'The disappearance of proper conduct means that, being unable to practise jhana, insight, the Ways and the fruits, they will guard no more the four entire purities of moral habit. As time goes on and on they will only guard the four offences entailing defeat. While there

73

are even a hundred or a thousand monks who guard and bear in mind the four offences entailing defeat, there will be no disappearance of proper conduct. With the breaking of moral habit by the last monk or on the extinction of his life, proper conduct will have disappeared.

'This, Sariputta, is the disappearance of proper conduct.

'The disappearance of learning means that as long as there stand firm the texts with the commentaries pertaining to the word of the Buddha in the three Pitakas, for so long there will be no disappearance of learning. As time goes on and on there will be base-born kings, not Dhamma-men; their ministers and so on will not be Dhamma-men, and consequently the inhabitants of the kingdom and so on will not be Dhamma-men. Because they are not Dhamma-men it will not rain properly. Therefore the crops will not flourish well, and in consequence the donors of requisites to the community of monks will not be able to give them the requisites. Not receiving the requisites the monks will not receive pupils. As time goes on and on learning will decay. In this decay the Great Patthanā itself will decay first. In this decay also (there will be) Yamaka, Kathāvatthu, Puggalapaññati, Dhātukathā, Vibhanga and Dhammasangani. When the Abhidhamma Pitaka decays the Suttanta Pitaka will decay. When the Suttantas decay the Anguttara will decay first. When it decays the Samyutta Nikāya, the Majjhima Nikāya, the Dīgha Nikāya and the Khuddaka-Nikāya will decay. They will simply remember the Jātaka together wit the Vinaya-Pitaka. But only the conscientious (monks) will remember the Vinaya-Pitaka. As time goes on and on, being unable to remember even the Jātaka, the Vessantara-jātaka will decay first. When that decays the Āpannaka-jātaka will decay. When the Jātakas decay they will remember only the Vinaya-Pitaka. As time goes on and on the Vinaya-Pitaka will decay. While a four-line stanza still continues to exist among men, there will not be a disappearance of learning. When a king who has faith has had a purse containing a thousand (coins) placed in a golden casket on an elephant's back, and has had the drum (of proclamation) sounded in the city up to the second or third time, to the effect that: "Whoever knows a stanza uttered by the Buddhas, let him take these thousand coins together with the royal elephant"—but yet finding no one knowing a four-line stanza, the purse containing the thousand (coins) must be taken back into the palace again—then will be the disappearance of learning.

'This, Sariputta, is the disappearance of learning.

'As time goes on and on each of the last monks, carrying his robe, bowl, and tooth-pick like Jain recluses, having taken a bottle-gourd and turned it into a bowl for almsfood, will wander about with it in his forearms or hands or hanging from a piece of string. As time goes on and on, thinking: "What's the good of this yellow robe?" and cutting off a small piece of one and sticking it on his nose or ear or in his hair, he will wander about supporting wife and children by agriculture, trade and the like. Then he will give a gift to the Southern community for those (of bad moral habit). I say that he will then acquire an incalculable fruit of the gift. As time goes on and on, thinking: "What's the good of this to us?", having thrown away the piece of yellow robe, he will harry beasts and birds in the forest. At this time the outward form will have disappeared.

'This, Sariputta, is called the disappearance of the outward form.

'Then when the Dispensation of the Perfect Buddha is 5,000 years old, the relics, not receiving reverence and honour, will go to places where they can receive them. As time goes on and on there will not be reverence and honour for them in every place. At the time when the Dispensation is falling into (oblivion), all the relics, coming from every place: from the abode of serpents and the deva-world and the Brahma-world, having gathered together in the space round the great Bo-tree, having made a Buddha-image, and having performed a "miracle" like the Twin-miracle, will teach Dhamma. No human being will be found at that place. All the devas of the ten-thousand world system, gathered together, will hear Dhamma and many thousands of them will attain to Dhamma. And these will cry aloud, saying: "Behold, devatas, a week from today our One of the Ten Powers will attain complete Nirvāna." They will weep, saying: "Henceforth there will be darkness for us." Then the relics, producing the condition of heat, will burn up that image leaving no remainder.

'This, Sariputta, is called the disappearance of the relics.'

Translation and explanatory material by Edward Conze, in Conze *et al.*, *Buddhist Texts through the Ages* (Oxford: Bruno Cassirer (Publishers) Ltd., 1954).

190. IRANIAN ESCHATOLOGY: THE RAISING OF THE DEAD AND THE FINAL BODY

(Greater Bundahishn)

(1) It is said in the Religion that just as Mashyē and Mashyānē, after they had grown out of the earth, consumed water first, then plants,

then milk, and then meat, so do men when they are [are about to] die, abstain first from the eating of meat and milk and then from bread; but right up to the moment of death they drink water.

(2) So too in the millennium of Oshētarmāh (the last millennium before the coming of Sōshyans) the power of Āz (gluttony) is so diminished that men are satisfied by eating one meal every three days and nights. After that they abstain from eating meat, and eat (only) plants and the milk of domestic animals. After that they abstain from drinking milk also; then they abstain from eating plants too, and drink only water. Ten years before the coming of Sōshyans they reach a state in which they eat nothing, yet do not die.

(3) Then Sōshyans will raise up the dead, as (the Religion) says, 'Zoroaster asked Ohrmazd, "From whence can the body which the wind has carried off and the water swept away, be put together again; and how will the raising of the dead come to pass?" And Ohrmazd made answer (and said): "When [I established] the sky without pillar on an invisible (*mēnōk*) support, its ends flung wide apart, bright with the substance of shining metal, and when I created the earth which supports the whole material creation though itself has no material support, and when I set the Sun, Moon, and stars—forms of light— on their courses in the atmosphere, and when I created grain on earth and scattered it abroad so that it grows up again and yields a greater crop, and when I created various and variegated colours in the plants, and when I gave fire to the plants and other things and it did not burn (them), and when I created the embryo in its mother's womb and gave it nourishment, giving to it its several organs, . . . when I created each one of these things, each was more difficult than the raising of the dead. For in the raising of the dead I have the assistance of the likes of these. When they were still [uncreated], I had [no such assistance].

(4) '"Behold! If I created what had not been, why should it be impossible for me to recreate what once was? For at that time I shall demand from the Spirit of the Earth the bones, from the water the blood, from the plants the hair, from the wind the spirit (*jān*) even as they received them at the primal creation." '

(5) First will be raised the bones of Gayōmart, then the bones of Mashyē and Mashyānē: then will the bones of (all) other men be raised up. For fifty-seven years will Sōshyans raise the dead and all men will be resurrected, both those who were saved and those who were damned. And each man will arise in the place where his spirit left him or where first he fell to the ground. . . .

(7) Then will men recognize each other, that is, soul will recognize soul and body (thinking), 'This is my father,' or 'This is my brother,' or 'This is my wife,' or 'This is whatever close relative it may be.' Then the assembly of Isat-vāstar will convene when men stand upon the earth in that assembly; and every man will see his good and evil deeds, and the saved will be as clearly distinguished from the damned as is a white sheep from a black.

(8) And in that assembly the damned man who had on earth a friend who was saved, will upbraid the man who was saved, saying, 'Why didst thou not apprise me on earth of the good deeds that thou thyself wast doing?' And if in truth the man who was saved did not so apprise him, then must he needs be put to shame in that assembly.

(9) Then will they separate the saved from the damned, and carry off the saved to Paradise (garōdhmān) and hurl the damned back into Hell; and for three days and nights these denizens of Hell will endure punishment in Hell, in their bodies and in their souls (jān) while the saved experience joy in their bodies during their three days and nights in Paradise.

(10) For it is said that on that day when damned is separated from saved, and saved from damned, tears will flow down from (the eyes of) all men, right down to their feet. When son is separated from the company of father, brother from brother, friend from friend, then will every man bewail the deeds he did, the saved weeping for the damned, and the damned weeping for themselves. It may be the father who is saved and the son who is damned, or it may be one brother who is saved and the other who is damned. . . .

(13) And Gōchihr, the serpent in the heavenly sphere, will fall from the summit of the Moon to the earth, and the earth will suffer pain like unto the pain a sheep feels when a wolf rends out its wool.

(14) Then will the Fire-god and the god Airyaman melt the metals that are in the mountains and hills, and they will flow over the earth like rivers. And they will make all men to pass through that molten metal and (thereby) make them clean. And it will seem to him who was saved as if he were walking through warm milk, but to the man who was damned it will seem exactly like walking through molten metal.

(15) Then will all men come together in the greatest joy, father and son, brothers and all friends. And one man will ask another, 'How has thy soul fared in all these many years? Wast thou saved, or wast thou damned?' Next the soul will see its body, will question it and be answered by it.

(16) All men will become of one voice and give praise with a loud

voice to Ohrmazd and the Amahraspands. At this time Ohrmazd will have brought his creation to its consummation, and there will be no (further) work he need do.

(17) While the resurrection of the dead proceeds, Sōshyans and his helpers will perform the sacrifice of the raising of the dead, and in that sacrifice the bull Hadhayans will be slain, and from the fat of the bull they will prepare the white Hōm (Haoma), (the drink of) immortality, and give it to all men. And all men will become immortal for ever and ever. . . .

(19) To each man his wife and children will be restored, and they will have intercourse with their wives even as they do on earth today, but no children will be born to them. . . .

(22) Then Ohrmazd will seize hold of the Destructive Spirit, Vahuman (the Good Mind) will seize Akōman (the Evil Mind), Artvahisht Indar, Shahrēvar Sāvul, Spandarmat Tarōmat (Arrogance) who is Nānghaith, Hurdāt and Amurdāt will seize Tairich and Zairich, True Speech False Speech, and the blessed Srōsh will seize upon Eshm (Wrath) of the bloody banner.

(23) Then (only) two Lies will remain, Ahriman and Āz (Concupiscence). Ohrmazd will come (down) to earth, himself the 'Zōt'-priest with the blessed Srōsh as his 'Raspik'-priest, and he will hold the sacred girdle in his hand. By that Gāthic ritual Ahriman and Āz, their weapons smashed, will be made powerless; and by the same passage through the sky by which they rushed in, they will hurtle into the darkness and gloom.

(24) And the serpent Gōchihr will be burnt up in the molten metal; and the molten metal will flow out into Hell. And (all) the stench and corruption that was in Hell will be burnt up by this molten metal and made clean. And [the hole in (?)] Hell by which the Destructive Spirit rushed in, will be sealed up by that molten metal, and the earth that was in Hell will be brought up to the broad expanse of (this) material world.

(25) Then will the final Resurrection take place in the two worlds; and in accordance with its own desire the material world will become immortal for ever and ever.

(26) This too is said, that this earth will become flat, with neither hills nor dales. There will be neither mountains nor ridges nor pits, neither high ground nor low.

Translation by R. C. Zaehner, in his *The Teachings of the Magi* (London, 1956), pp. 145-50; from *Bundahishn* (edited by Anklesaria), pp. 220-8

The End of the World

191. MUHAMMAD SPEAKS OF THE DAY OF DOOM

('Koran,' LVI, 1-55; LXIX, 14-39)

In the Name of God, the Merciful, the Compassionate

When the Terror descends
(and none denies its descending)
abasing, exalting,
when the earth shall be rocked
and the mountains crumbled
and become a dust scattered,
and you shall be three bands—

Companions of the Right (O Companions of the Right!)
Companions of the Left (O Companions of the Left!)
and the Outstrippers: the Outstrippers
those are they brought nigh the Throne,
in the Gardens of Delight
(a throng of the ancients
and how few of the later folk)
upon close-wrought couches
reclining upon them, set face to face,
immortal youths going round about them
with goblets, and ewers, and a cup from a spring
(no brows throbbing, no intoxication)
and such fruits as they shall choose,
and such flesh of fowl as they desire,
and wide-eyed houris
as the likeness of hidden pearls,
a recompense for that they laboured.
Therein they shall hear no idle talk, no cause of sin,
only the saying 'Peace, Peace!'

The Companions of the Right (O Companions of the Right!)
mid thornless lote-trees and serried acacias,
and spreading shade and outpoured waters,
and fruits abounding
unfailing, unforbidden,
and upraised couches.

Perfectly We formed them, perfect,
and We made them spotless virgins,
   chastely amorous, like of age
for the Companions of the Right.
   A throng of the ancients
and a throng of the later folk.

The Companions of the Left (O Companions of the Left!)
   mid burning winds and boiling waters
   and the shadow of a smoking blaze
     neither cool, neither goodly;
   and before that they lived at ease,
    and persisted in the Great Sin,
      ever saying,
   'What, when we are dead and become
   dust and bones, shall we indeed
    be raised up?
   What, and our fathers, the ancients?'

Say: 'The ancients, and the later folk
shall be gathered to the appointed time
   of a known day.
Then you erring ones, you that cried lies,
you shall eat of a tree called Zakkoum,
and you shall fill therewith your bellies
and drink on top of that boiling water
lapping it down like thirsty camels.
This shall be their hospitality on the
   Day of Doom. (LVI, 1-55.)

So, when the Trumpet is blown with a single blast
and the earth and the mountains are lifted up and
    crushed with a single blow,
then, on that day, the Terror shall come to pass,
and heaven shall be split, for upon that day it
    shall be very frail,
and the angels shall stand upon its borders, and
upon that day eight shall carry above them the
    Throne of thy Lord.
On that day you shall be exposed, not one secret
   of yours concealed.

The End of the World

Then as for him who is given his book in his right hand,
he shall say, 'Here, take and read my book! Certainly
I thought that I should encounter my reckoning.' So he
     shall be in a pleasing life
     in a lofty Garden,
     its clusters nigh to gather.
'Eat and drink with wholesome appetite for that you did
     long ago, in the days gone by.'
But as for him who is given his book in his left hand,
he shall say, 'Would that I had not been given my book
and not known my reckoning! Would it had been the end!
     My wealth has not availed me,
     my authority is gone from me.'
Take him, and fetter him, and then roast him in Hell,
then in a chain of seventy cubits' length insert him!
Behold, he never believed in God the All-mighty, and
he never urged the feeding of the needy; therefore he
today has not here one loyal friend, neither any food
saving foul pus, that none excepting the sinners eat.

                                          (LXIX, 41-39.)

               Translation by A. J. Arberry

J. MESSIANIC PROPHECIES AND MILLENARIAN MOVEMENTS

('Maitreyavyākarana')

Maitreya will appear in the future, some thirty thousand years hence. At present Maitreya is believed to reside in the Tushita heaven, awaiting his last rebirth when the time is ripe. His name is derived from mitra, 'friend,' friendliness being a basic Buddhist virtue, akin to Christian love.

Sariputra, the great general of the doctrine, most wise and resplendent, from compassion for the world asked the Lord: 'Some time ago you have spoken to us of the future Buddha, who will lead the world at a future period, and who will bear the name of Maitreya. I would now wish to hear more about his powers and miraculous gifts. Tell me, O best of men, about them!'

The Lord replied: 'At that time, the ocean will lose much of its water, and there will be much less of it than now. In consequence a world-ruler will have no difficulties in passing across it. India, this island of Jambu, will be quite flat everywhere, it will measure ten thousand leagues, and all men will have the privilege of living on it. It will have innumerable inhabitants, who will commit no crimes or evil deeds, but will take pleasure in doing good. The soil will then be free from thorns, even, and covered with a fresh green growth of grass; when one jumps on it, it gives way, and becomes soft like the leaves of the cotton tree. It has a delicious scent, and tasty rice grows on it, without any work. Rich silken, and other, fabrics of various colours shoot forth from the trees. The trees will bear leaves, flowers, and fruits simultaneously; they are as high as the voice can reach and they last for eight myriads of years. Human beings are then without any blemishes, moral offences are unknown among them, and they are full of zest and joy. Their bodies are very large and their skin has a fine hue. Their strength is quite extraordinary. Three kinds of illness only are known—people must relieve their bowels, they must eat, they must get old. Only when five hundred years old do the women marry.

'The city of Ketumatī will at that time be the capital. In it will reside the world-ruler, Shankha by name, who will rule over the earth up to the confines of the ocean; and he will make the Dharma prevail. He will be a great hero, raised to his station by the force of hundreds of meritorious deeds. His spiritual adviser will be a Brahmin, Subrahmana by name, a very learned man, well versed in the four Vedas, and steeped in all the lore of the Brahmins. And that Brahman will have a wife, called Brahmavatī, beautiful, attractive, handsome, and renowned.

'Maitreya, the best of men, will then leave the Tushita heavens, and go for his last rebirth into the womb of that woman. For ten whole months she will carry about his radiant body. Then she will go to a grove full of beautiful flowers, and there, neither seated nor lying down, but standing up, holding on to the branch of a tree, she will give birth to Maitreya. He, supreme among men, will emerge from her right side, as the sun shines forth when it has prevailed over a bank of clouds. No more polluted by the impurities of the womb than a lotus by drops of water, he will fill this entire Triple world with his splendour. As soon as he is born he will walk seven steps forward, and where he puts down his feet a jewel or a lotus will spring up. He will raise his eyes to the ten directions, and will speak these words: "This is my last birth. There will be no rebirth after this one. Never will I come back here, but, all pure, I shall win Nirvāna!"

'And when his father sees that his son has the thirty-two marks of a superman, and considers their implications in the light of the holy mantras, he will be filled with joy, for he will know that, as the mantras show, two ways are open to his son: he will either be a universal monarch, or a supreme Buddha. But as Maitreya grows up, the Dharma will increasingly take possession of him, and he will reflect that all that lives is bound to suffer. He will have a heavenly voice which reaches far; his skin will have a golden hue, a great splendour will radiate from his body, his chest will be broad, his limbs well developed, and his eyes will be like lotus petals. His body is eighty cubits high, and twenty cubits broad. He will have a retinue of 84,000 persons, whom he will instruct in the mantras. With this retinue he will one day go forth into the homeless life. A Dragon tree will then be the tree under which he will win enlightenment; its branches rise up to fifty leagues, and its foliage spreads far and wide over six Kos. Underneath it Maitreya, the best of men, will attain enlightenment—

there can be no doubt on that. And he will win his enlightenment the very same day that he has gone forth into the homeless life.

'And then, a supreme sage, he will with a perfect voice preach the true Dharma, which is auspicious and removes all ill, i.e. the fact of ill, the origination of ill, the transcending of ill, and the holy eightfold path which brings security and leads to Nirvāna. He will explain the four Truths, because he has seen that generation, in faith, ready for them, and those who have listened to his Dharma will thereupon make progress in the religion. They will be assembled in a park full of beautiful flowers, and his assembly will extend over a hundred leagues. Under Maitreya's guidance, hundreds of thousands of living beings shall enter upon a religious life.

'And thereupon Maitreya, the compassionate teacher, surveys those who have gathered around him, and speaks to them as follows: "Shākyamuni has seen all of you, he, the best of sages, the saviour, the world's true protector, the repository of the true Dharma. It was he who has set you on the path to deliverance, but before you could finally win it you have had to wait for my teaching. It is because you have worshipped Shākyamuni with parasols, banners, flags, perfumes, garlands, and unguents that you have arrived here to hear my teaching. It is because you have offered to the shrines of Shākyamuni unguents of sandalwood, or powdered saffron, that you have arrived here to hear my teaching. It is because you have always gone for refuge to the Buddha, the Dharma, and the Samgha, that you have arrived here to hear my teaching. It is because, in Shākyamuni's dispensation, you have undertaken to observe the moral precepts, and have actually done so, that you have arrived here to hear my teaching. It is because you have given gifts to the monks —robes, drink, food, and many kinds of medicines—that you have arrived here to hear my teaching. It is because you have always observed the sabbath days that you have arrived here to hear my teaching.". . .

'For 60,000 years Maitreya, the best of men, will preach the true Dharma, which is compassionate towards all living beings. And when he has disciplined in his true Dharma hundreds and hundreds of millions of living beings, then that leader will at last enter Nirvāna. And after the great sage has entered Nirvāna, his true Dharma still endures for another ten thousand years.

'Raise therefore your thoughts in faith to Shākyamuni, the Conqueror! For then you shall see Maitreya, the perfect Buddha, the best of men! Whose soul could be so dark that it would not be lit up with a serene faith when he hears these wonderful things, so potent of future good! Those therefore who long for spiritual greatness, let them show respect to the true Dharma, let them be mindful of the religion of the Buddhas!'

Translation by Edward Conze, in his *Buddhist Scriptures* (Penguin Books, 1959), pp. 238-42

193. NICHIREN SEES JAPAN AS THE CENTRE OF BUDDHISM'S REGENERATION

Nichiren (1222-82) was a Japanese religious teacher who established a Buddhist sect.

When, at a certain future time, the union of the state law and the Buddhist Truth shall be established, and the harmony between the two completed, both sovereign and subjects will faithfully adhere to the Great Mysteries. Then the golden age, such as were the ages under the reign of the sage kings of old, will be realized in these days of degeneration and corruption, in the time of the Latter Law. Then the establishment of the Holy See will be completed, by imperial grant and the edict of the Dictator, at a spot comparable in its excellence with the Paradise of Vulture Peak. We have only to wait for the coming of the time. Then the moral law *(kaihō)* will be achieved in the actual life of mankind. The Holy See will be the seat where all men of the three countries [India, China and Japan] and the whole Jambudvīpa [world] will be initiated into the mysteries of confession and expiation; and even the great deities, Brahmā and Indra, will come down into the sanctuary and participate in the initiation.

Masaharu Anesaki, *Nichiren, the Buddhist Prophet* (Cambridge, Mass., 1916), p. 110; as quoted in Wm. Theodore de Bary (ed.), *Sources of Japanese Tradition* (New York: Columbia University Press, 1958), p. 230

194. A SIOUX NATIVISTIC MOVEMENT: THE GHOST-DANCE RELIGION

The great underlying principle of the Ghost dance doctrine is that the time will come when the whole Indian race, living and dead, will be reunited upon a regenerated earth, to live a life of aboriginal happiness, forever free from death, disease, and misery. On this foundation each tribe has built a structure from its own mythology, and each apostle and believer has filled in the details according to his own mental capacity or ideas of happiness, with such additions as come to him from the trance. Some changes, also, have undoubtedly resulted from the transmission of the doctrine through the imperfect medium of the sign language. . . .

All this is to be brought about by overruling spiritual power that needs no assistance from human creatures; and though certain medicine-men were disposed to anticipate the Indian millennium by preaching resistance to the further encroachments of the whites, such teachings form no part of the true doctrine, and it was only where chronic dissatisfaction was aggravated by recent grievances, as among the Sioux, that the movement assumed a hostile expression. On the contrary, all believers were exhorted to make themselves worthy of the predicted happiness by discarding all things warlike and practising honesty, peace, and good will, not only among themselves, but also toward the whites, so long as they were together. Some apostles have even thought that all race distinctions are to be obliterated, and that the whites are to participate with the Indians in the coming felicity; but it seems unquestionable that this is equally contrary to the doctrine as originally preached.

Different dates have been assigned at various times for the fulfillment of the prophecy. Whatever the year, it has generally been held, for very natural reasons, that the regeneration of the earth and the renewal of all life would occur in the early spring. In some cases July, and particularly the 4th of July, was the expected time. This, it may be noted, was about the season when the great annual ceremony of the sun dances formerly took place among the prairie tribes. The messiah himself has set several dates from time to time, as one prediction after another failed to materialize, and in his message to the Cheyenne and Arapaho, in August, 1891, he leaves the whole matter an open question. The date universally recognized among all the tribes immediately prior to the Sioux outbreak was the spring of 1891. As springtime came and passed, and summer grew and waned, and autumn faded again into winter without the realization of their hopes and longings, the doctrine gradually assumed its present form—that some time in the unknown future the Indian will be united with his friends who have gone before, to be forever supremely happy, and that this happiness may be anticipated in dreams, if not actually hastened in reality, by earnest and frequent attendance on the sacred dance. . . .

As I had always shown a sympathy for their ideas and feelings, and had now accomplished a long journey to the messiah himself at the cost of considerable difficulty and hardship, the Indians were at last fully satisfied that I was really desirous of learning the truth concerning their new religion. A few days after my visit to Left Hand, several of the delegates who had been sent out in the preceding August came down to see me, headed by Black Short Nose, a Cheyenne. After preliminary greetings, he stated that the Cheyenne and Arapaho were now convinced that I would tell the truth about their religion, and as they loved their religion and were anxious to have the whites know that it was all good and contained nothing bad or hostile they would now give me the message which the messiah himself had given to them, that I might take it back to show to Washington. He then took from a beaded pouch and gave to me a letter, which proved to be the message or statement of the doctrine delivered by Wovoka to the Cheyenne and Arapaho delegates, of whom Black Short Nose was one, on the occasion of their last visit to Nevada, in August, 1891, and written down on the spot, in broken English, by one of the Arapaho delegates, Caspar Edson, a young man who had acquired some English education by several years' attendance at the government Indian school at Carlisle, Pennsylvania. On the reverse page of the paper was a duplicate in somewhat better English, written out by a daughter of Black Short Nose, a school girl, as dictated by her father on his return. These letters contained the message to be delivered to the two tribes, and as is expressly stated in the text were not intended to be seen by a white man. The daughter of Black Short Nose had attempted to erase this clause before her father brought the letter down to me, but the lines were still plainly visible. It is the genuine official statement of the Ghost-dance doctrine as given by the messiah himself to his disciples. . . .

The Messiah Letter (free rendering)

When you get home you must make a dance to continue five days. Dance four successive nights, and the last night keep up the dance until the morning of the fifth day, when all must bathe in the river and then disperse to their homes. You must all do in the same way.

I, Jack Wilson, love you all, and my heart is full of gladness for the gifts you have brought me. When you get home I shall give you a good cloud [rain?] which will make you feel good. I give you a good spirit and give you all good paint. I want you to come again in three months, some from each tribe there [the Indian Territory].

There will be a good deal of snow this year and some rain. In the fall there will be such a rain as I have never given you before.

Grandfather [a universal title or reverence among Indians and here meaning the messiah] says, when your friends die you must not cry. You must not hurt anybody or do harm to anyone. You must not fight. Do right always. It will give you satisfaction in life. This young man has a good father and mother. [Possibly this refers to Casper Edson, the young Arapaho who wrote down this message of Wovoka for the delegation].

Do not tell the white people about this. Jesus is now upon the earth. He appears like a cloud. The dead are alive all again. I do not know when they will be here; maybe this fall or in the spring. When the time comes there will be no more sickness and everyone will be young again.

Do not refuse to work for the whites and do not make any trouble with them until you leave them. When the earth shakes [at the coming of the new world] do not be afraid. It will not hurt you.

I want you to dance every six weeks. Make a feast at the dance and have food that everybody may eat. Then bathe in the water. That is all. You will receive good words again from me some time. Do not tell lies.

The mythology of the doctrine is only briefly indicated, but the principal articles are given. The dead are all risen and the spirit hosts are advancing and have already arrived at the boundaries of this earth, led forward by the regenerator in shape of cloud-like indistinctness. The spirit captain of the dead is always represented under this shadowy semblance. The great change will be ushered in by a trembling of the earth, at which the faithful are exhorted to feel no alarm. The hope held out is the same that has inspired the Christian for nineteen centuries—a happy immortality in perpetual youth. As to fixing a date, the messiah is as cautious as his predecessor in prophecy, who declares that 'no man knoweth the time, not even the angels of God.' His weather predictions also are about as definite as the inspired utterances of the Delphian oracle. . . .

We may now consider details of the doctrine as held by different tribes, beginning with the Paiute, among whom it originated. The best account of the Paiute belief is contained in a report to the War Department by Captain J. M. Lee, who was sent out in the autumn of 1890 to investigate the temper and fighting strength of the Paiute and other Indians in the vicinity of Fort Bidwell in northeastern California. We give the statement obtained by him from Captain Dick, a Paiute, as delivered one day in a conversational way and apparently without reserve, after nearly all the Indians had left the room:

'Long time, twenty years ago, Indian medicine-man in Mason's valley at Walker lake talk same way, same as you hear now. In one year, maybe, after he begin talk he die. Three years ago another medicine-man begin same talk. Heap talk all time. Indians hear about it everywhere. Indians come from long way off to hear him. They come from the east; they make signs. Two years ago me go to Winnemucca and Pyramid lake, me see Indian Sam, a head man, and Johnson Sides. Sam he tell me he just been to see Indian medicine-man to hear him talk. Sam say medicine-man talk this way:

' "All Indians must dance, everywhere, keep on dancing. Pretty soon in next spring Big Man [Great Spirit] come. He bring back all game of every kind. The game be thick everywhere. All dead Indians come back and live again. They all be strong just like young man, be young again. Old blind Indian see again and get young and have fine time. When Old Man [God] comes this way, then all the Indians go to mountains, high up away from whites. Whites can't hurt Indians then. Then while Indians way up high, big flood comes like water and all white people die, get drowned. After that water go way and then nobody but Indians everywhere and game all kinds thick. Then medicine-man tell Indians to send word to all Indians to keep up dancing and the good time will come. Indians who don't dance, who don't believe in this word, will grow little, just about a foot high, and stay that way. Some of them will be turned into wood and be burned in fire." That's the way Sam tell me the medicine-man talk.'

Lieutenant N. P. Phister, who gathered a part of the material embodied in Captain Lee's report, confirms this general statement and gives a few additional particulars. The flood is to consist of mingled mud and water, and when the faithful go up into the mountains, the sceptics will be left behind and will be turned to stone. The prophet claims to receive these revelations directly from God and the spirits of the dead Indians during his trances. He asserts also that he is invulnerable, and that if soldiers should attempt to kill him they would fall down as if they had no bones and die, while he would still live, even though cut into little pieces.

One of the first and most prominent of those who brought the doctrine to the prairie tribes was Porcupine, a Cheyenne, who crossed the mountains with several companions in the fall of 1889, visited Wovoka, and attended the dance near Walker Lake, Nevada. In his report of his experiences, made some months later to a military officer, he states that Wovoka claimed to be Christ himself, who had come back again, many centuries after his first rejection, in pity to teach his children. He quoted the prophet as saying:

'I found my children were bad, so I went back to heaven and left them. I told them that in so many hundred years I would come back to see my children. At the end of this time I was sent back to try to teach them. My father told me the earth was getting old and worn out and the people getting bad, and that I was to renew everything as it used to be and make it better.

'He also told us that all our dead were to be resurrected; that they were all to come back to earth, and that, as the earth was too small for them and us, he would do away with heaven and make the earth itself large enough to contain us all; that we must tell all the people we met about these things. He spoke to us about fighting; and said that was bad and we must keep from it; that the earth was to be all good hereafter, and we must all be friends with one another. He said that in the fall of the year the youth of all good people would be renewed, so that nobody would be more than forty years old, and that if they behaved themselves well after this the youth of everyone would be renewed in the spring. He said if we were all good he would send people among us who could heal all our wounds and sickness by mere touch and that we would live forever. He told us not to quarrel or fight or strike each other, or shoot one another; that the whites and Indians were to be all one people. He said if any man disobeyed what he ordered his tribe would be wiped from the face of the earth; that we must believe everything he said, and we must not doubt him or say he lied; that if we did, he would know it; that he would know our thoughts and actions in no matter what part of the world we might be.'

Here we have the statement that both races are to live together as one. We have also the doctrine of healing by touch. Whether or not this is an essential part of the system is questionable, but it is certain that the faithful believe that great physical good comes to them, to their children, and to the sick from the imposition of hands by the priests of the dance, apart from the ability thus conferred to see the things of the spiritual world.

Another idea here presented, namely, that the earth becomes old and decrepit, and requires that its youth be renewed at the end of certain great cycles, is common to a number of tribes, and has an important place in the oldest religions of the world. As an Arapaho who spoke English expressed it, 'This earth too old, grass too old, trees too old, our lives too old. Then all be new again.' Captain H. L. Scott also found among the southern plains tribes the same belief that the rivers, the mountains, and the earth itself are worn out and must be renewed, together with an indefinite idea that both races alike must die at the same time, to be resurrected in new but separate worlds. . . .

The manner of the final change and the destruction of the whites has been variously interpreted as the doctrine was carried from its original centre. East of the mountains it is commonly held that a deep sleep will come on the believers, during which the great catastrophe will be accomplished, and the faithful will awake to immortality on a new earth. The Shoshoni of Wyoming say this sleep will continue four nights and days, and that on the morning of the fifth day all will open their eyes in a new world where both races will dwell together forever. The Cheyenne, Arapaho, Kiowa, and others, of Oklahoma, say that the new earth, with all the resurrected dead from the beginning, and with the buffalo, the elk, and other game upon it, will come from the west and slide over the surface of the present earth, as the right hand might slide over the left. As it approaches, the Indians will be carried upward and alight on it by the aid of the sacred dance feather which they wear in their hair and which will act as wings to bear them up. They will then become unconscious for four days, and on waking out of their trance will find themselves with their former friends in the midst of all the old time surroundings. By Sitting Bull, the Arapaho apostle, it is thought that this new earth as it advances will be preceded by a wall of fire which will drive the whites across the water to their original and proper country, while the Indians will be enabled by means of the sacred feathers to surmount the flames and reach the promised land. When the expulsion of the whites has been accomplished, the fire will be extinguished by a rain continuing twelve days. By a few it is believed that a hurricane with thunder and lightning will come to destroy the whites alone. This last idea is said to be held also by the Walapai of Arizona, who extend its provisions to include the unbelieving Indians as well. The doctrine held by the Caddo, Wichita, and Delaware, of Oklahoma, is practically the same as is held by the Arapaho and Cheyenne from whom they obtained it. All these tribes believe that the destruction or removal of the whites is to be accomplished entirely by supernatural means, and they severely blame the Sioux for having provoked a physical conflict by their impatience instead of waiting for their God to deliver them in his own good time.

Among all the tribes which have accepted the new faith it is held that frequent devout attendance on the dance conduces to ward off disease and restore the sick to health, this applying not only to the actual participants, but also to their children and friends. The idea of obtaining temporal blessings as the reward of a faithful performance of religious duties is too natural and universal to require comment. The purification by the sweat-bath, which forms an important preliminary to the dance among the Sioux, while devotional in its purpose, is probably also sanitary in its effect.

Among the powerful and warlike Sioux of the Dakotas, already restless under both old and recent grievances, and more lately brought to the edge of starvation by a reduction of rations, the doctrine speedily assumed a hostile meaning and developed some peculiar features, for which reason it deserves particular notice as concerns this tribe. The earliest rumours of the new messiah came to the Sioux from the more western tribes in the winter of 1888-89, but the first definite account was brought by a delegation which crossed the mountains to visit the messiah in the fall of 1889, returning in the spring of 1890. On the report of these delegates the dance was at once inaugurated and spread so rapidly that in a few months the new religion had been accepted by the majority of the tribe.

Perhaps the best statement of the Sioux version is given by the veteran agent, James McLaughlin, of Standing Rock Agency. In an official letter of October 17, 1890, he writes that the Sioux, under the influence of Sitting Bull, were greatly excited over the near approach of a predicted Indian millennium or 'return of the ghosts,' when the white man would be annihilated and the Indian again supreme, and which the medicine-men had promised was to occur as soon as the grass was green in the spring. They were told that the Great Spirit had sent upon them the dominant race to punish them for their sins, and that their sins were now expiated and the time of deliverance was at hand. Their decimated ranks were to be reinforced by all the Indians who had ever died, and these spirits were already on their way to reinhabit the earth, which had originally belonged to the Indians, and were driving before them, as they advanced, immense herds of buffalo and fine ponies. The Great Spirit, who had so long deserted his red children, was now once more with them and against the whites, and the white man's gunpowder would no longer have power to drive a bullet through the skin of an Indian. The whites themselves would soon be overwhelmed and smothered under a deep landslide, held down by sod and timber, and the few who might escape would become small fishes in the rivers. In order to bring about this happy result, the Indians must believe and organize the Ghost dance.

James Mooney, *The Ghost-Dance Religion and the Sioux Outbreak of 1890*, Fourteenth Annual Report, part 2, Bureau of American Ethnology (Washington, D.C., 1896), pp. 641-1110; quotation from pp. 777-87

195. THE GHOST-DANCE RELIGION (SIOUX): THE CEREMONY

The dance commonly begins about the middle of the afternoon or later, after sundown. When it begins in the afternoon, there is always an intermission of an hour or two for supper. The announcement is made by the criers, old men who assume this office apparently by tacit understanding, who go about the camp shouting in a loud voice to the people to prepare for the dance. The preliminary painting and dressing is usually a work of about two hours. When all is ready, the leaders walk out to the dance place, and facing inward, join hands so as to form a small circle. Then, without moving from their places they sing the opening song, according to previous agreement, in a soft undertone. Having sung it through once more they raise their voices to their full strength and repeat it, this time slowly circling around in the dance. The step is different from that of most other Indian dances, but very simple, the dancers moving from right to left, following the course of the sun, advancing the left foot and following it with the right, hardly lifting the feet from the ground. For this reason it is called by the Shoshoni the 'dragging dance.' All the songs are adapted to the simple measure of the dance step. As the song rises and swells the people come singly and in groups from the several tipis, and one after another joins the circle until any number from fifty to five hundred men, women, and children are in the dance. When the circle is small, each song is repeated through a number of circuits. If large, it is repeated only through one circuit, measured by the return of the leaders to the starting point. Each song is started in the same manner, first in an undertone while the singers stand still in their places, and then with full voice as they begin to circle around. At intervals between the songs, more especially after the trances have begun, the dancers unclasp hands and sit down to smoke or talk for a few minutes. At such times the leaders sometimes deliver short addresses or sermons, or relate the recent trance experience of the dancer. In holding each other's hands the dancers usually intertwine the fingers instead of grasping the the hand as with us. Only an Indian could keep the blanket in place as they do under such circumstances. Old people hobbling along with sticks, and little children hardly past the toddling period sometimes form a part of the circle, the more vigorous dancers accommodating the movement to their weakness. Frequently a woman will be seen to join the circle with an infant upon her back and dance with the others, but should she show the least sign of approaching excitement watchful friends lead her away that no harm may come to the child. Dogs are driven off from the neighbourhood of the circle lest they should run against any of those who have fallen into a trance and thus awaken them. The dancers themselves are careful not to disturb the trance subjects while their souls are in the spirit world. Full Indian dress is worn, with buckskin, paint, and feathers, but among the Sioux the women discarded the belts ornamented with discs of German silver, because the metal had come from the white man. Among the southern tribes, on the contrary, hats are sometimes worn in the dance, although this was not considered in strict accordance with the doctrine.

No drum, rattle, or other musical instrument is used in the dance, excepting sometimes by an individual dancer in imitation of a trance vision. In this respect particularly the Ghost dance differs from every other Indian dance. Neither are any fires built within the circle, so far as known, with any tribe excepting the Walapai. The northern Cheyenne, however, built four fires in a peculiar fashion outside of the circle, as already described. With most tribes the dance was performed around a tree or pole planted in the centre and variously decorated. In the southern plains, however, only the Kiowa seem ever to have followed this method, they sometimes dancing around a cedar tree. On breaking the circle at the end of the dance the performers shook their blankets or shawls in the air, with the idea of driving away all evil influences. On later instructions from the messiah all then went down to bathe in the stream, the men in one place and the women in another, before going to their tipis. The idea of washing away evil things, spiritual as well as earthly, by bathing in running water is too natural and universal to need comment. . . .

The most important feature of the Ghost dance, and the secret of the trances, is hypnotism. . . . Immediately on coming among the Arapaho and Cheyenne in 1890, I heard numerous stories of wonderful things that occurred in the Ghost dance—how people died, went to heaven and came back again, and how they talked with dead friends and brought back messages from the other world. Quite a number who had thus 'died' were mentioned and their adventures in the spirit land were related with great particularity of detail, but as most of the testimony came from white men, none of whom had seen the dance for themselves, I preserved the scientific attitude of scepticism. So far as could be ascertained, none of the intelligent people of the agency had thought the subject sufficiently worthy of serious consideration to learn whether the reports were true or false. On talking with the Indians I found them unanimous in their statements as to the visions, until I began to think there might be something in it.

The first clue to the explanation came from the statement of his own experience in the trance, given by Paul Boynton, a particularly bright Carlisle student, who acted as my interpreter. His brother had died some time before, and as Paul was anxious to see and talk with him, which the new doctrine taught was possible, he attended the next Ghost dance, and putting his hands upon the head of Sitting Bull, according to the regular formula, asked him to help him see his dead brother. Paul is of an inquiring disposition, and, besides his natural longing to meet his brother again, was actuated, as he himself said, by a desire to try 'every Indian trick.' He then told how Sitting Bull had hypnotized him with the eagle feather and the motion of his hands, until he fell unconscious and did really see his brother, but awoke just as he was about to speak to him, probably because one of the dancers had accidentally brushed against him as he lay on the ground. He embodied his experience in a song which was afterward sung in the dance. From his account it seemed almost certain that the secret was hypnotism.

> James Mooney, *The Ghost-Dance Religion and the Sioux Outbreak of 1890*, Fourteenth Annual Report, part 2, Bureau of American Ethnology (Washington, D.C., 1896), pp. 920-3

196. JOHN FRUM: A MILLENARIAN MOVEMENT IN TANNA, NEW HEBRIDES

Millenarian tendencies had been noted just before the turn of the century, when there had been rumours that Jesus would descend and lead the Christians to Heaven while Tanna and the pagans were consumed by fire. But the first important signs of native unrest did not become apparent until much later. In early 1940, there were signs of disturbance, exacerbated no doubt by a fall in copra prices. Meetings were held from which Whites were excluded, as were women. These meetings were to receive the message of one John Frum (spelt sometimes Jonfrum), described as a 'mysterious little man with bleached hair, high-pitched voice and clad in a coat with shining buttons.' He used 'ingenious stage-management . . . appearing at night, in the faint light of a fire, before men under the influence of kava.' John Frum issued pacific moral injunctions against idleness, encouraged communal gardening and co-operation, and advocated dancing and kava-drinking. He had no anti-White message at first and prophesied on traditional lines.

The prophet was regarded as the representative or earthly manifestation of Karaperamun, god of the island's highest mountain, Mount Tukosmeru. Karaperamun now appeared as John Frum, who was to be hidden from the Whites and from women.

John Frum prophesied the occurrence of a cataclysm in which Tanna would become flat, the volcanic mountains would fall and fill the river-beds to form fertile plains, and Tanna would be joined to the neighbouring islands of Eromanga and Aneityum to form a new island. Then John Frum would reveal himself, bringing in a reign of bliss, the natives would get back their youth, and there would be no sickness; there would be no need to care for gardens, trees or pigs. The Whites would go; John Frum would set up schools to replace mission schools, and would pay chiefs and teachers.

Only one difficulty prevented the immediate attainment of this happy state—the presence of the Whites, who had to be expelled first. The use of European money was also to cease. A corollary was the restoration of many ancient customs prohibited by the missionaries; kava-drinking above all, and also dancing, polygyny, etc. Immigrants from other islands were to be sent home.

This was not simply a programme of 'regression.' Only some of the ancient customs were to be revived, and they were customs banned by the missions. And the future envisaged was not the restoration of primitive tribalism and hand-agriculture, but a new life with 'all the material riches of the Europeans' accruing to the natives. John Frum would provide all the money needed.

Natives now started a veritable orgy of spending in European stores in order to get rid of the Europeans' money, which was to be replaced by John Frum's with a coconut stamped on it. Some even hurled their long-hoarded savings into the sea, believing that 'when there would be no money left on the island the White traders would have to depart, as no possible outlet would be found for their activity.' Lavish feasts were also held to use up food. There was thus no puritan or medieval-European 'asceticism' in these general joyful expectations of plenty. Rather, solidarity between rich and poor alike was expressed in this orgy of consumption, since, existing wealth was meaningless in the light of the prodigious riches to come. Friday, the day on which the millenium was expected, became a holy day, whilst on Saturday dances and kava-drinking took place. 'A certain licence accompanied the festivals,' Guiart remarks. We may be sure that this represents some socially-recognized breaking of existing conventions.

The movement was organized through messengers known as 'ropes of John Frum.' The enthusiasts broke away from the existing Christian villages which the missions had set up under Christian chiefs, and broke up into small family units living in 'primitive shelters,' or else joined pagan groups in the interior. This development, though formally the opposite of Santoese domestic communism, symbolizes the same basic social fact: a break with the mission-controlled villages and the old pattern of group life.

The first John Frum wave in April 1940 occasioned little alarm, but the revival of the movement in May 1941 created considerable perturbation. Large amounts of money were suddenly brought in by natives. Even gold sovereigns, which had not been seen since 1912 when they were paid to the chiefs who accepted the authority of the Government, appeared; this perhaps symbolized renunciation of the agreement. Some natives came in with over £100 in cash; cows and pigs were killed, kava drunk, and there was all-night dancing at the Green Point villages on the west coast where the movement had its centre. The Presbyterian missions, on Sunday the eleventh of May, found their services unattended. One of the most influencial chiefs had given the order to abandon the mission and their schools. Dominican services were equally neglected.

After a lapse of a week, Nicol [the British Agent] visited Green Point, only to find it empty except for a few women and children. He summoned twenty police reinforcements from Vila and, with the aid of one of the chiefs, arrested the John Frum leaders. A menacing crowd followed him shouting 'Hold firm for John Frum!'

In the trial, it transpired that John Frum was a native named Manehivi in his mid-thirties. He was illiterate (though he pretended to read), and refused to say where he had obtained his gold-buttoned coat. Manehivi was sentenced to three years' internment, and five years' exile from Tanna; nine others received a year's imprisonment, Nicol had Manehivi tied to a tree and exposed as an imposter for a day, and made five chiefs sign a statement asserting that they renounced John Frum, and fined him £100.

The movement still flourished in spite of repression. December 1941 was the significant date of the next major outbreak. News of Pearl Harbour had percolated through even to the natives of Tanna, though the defeat was credited to the Germans, who were going to win. Because of growing anti-British feeling, Nicol had twenty men arrested and sent to Vila, and recommended the establishment of a permanent police force.

Meanwhile the John Frum leaders in Vila were active. Manehivi was not the real John Frum, people said; the latter was still at large. Missionaries intercepted messages written from Vila by a second John Frum, a Tama police-boy, Joe Nalpin, and addressed to a west coast chief and two other men. They contained a new theme: John Frum was King of America, or would send his son to America to seek the King, or his son was coming from America, or his sons were to seek John Frum in America. Mount Tukosmeru would be 'covered by invisible planes belonging to John Frum.' Nalpin actually helped to direct the new phase from gaol, where he was serving a nine months' sentence.

In January, Australian Cataline flyingboats on patrol were the probable origin of the rumour that three sons of John Frum—Isaac, Jacob and Lastuan (Last-One?)—had landed by plane on the other side of the island from Green Point. 'Junketings' were going on night and day, as it was believed that John Frum's advent was imminent. The appearance of the first Americans and of numerous planes added fuel to the flames. . . .

As the Americans moved in to meet the Japanese threat, the news of their arrival swept the islands. A man was arrested for saying that Mount Tukomeru was 'full of soldiers'; it would open on the Day, and the soldiers would fight for John Frum. But the most astounding piece of information was the news that many of these U.S. troops were *black!* It was prophesied that large numbers of black Americans were coming to rule over the natives. Their dollars would become the new money; they would release the prisoners, and pay wages.

Consequently, the Americans met with a splendid response when they set out to hire native labour. The movement now revived on Tanna, and kava-drinking and dancing were the order of the day, especially on the east coast; the missions were still boycotted. More arrests were made, and the prisoners sent to Vila, where many were allowed to work for the U.S. Air Force. . . .

In October, Nicol returned. His arrival precipitated a new John Frum demonstration which was broken up by the police. Natives armed with guns and clubs resisted arrest and reinforcements were summoned. A new leader in the north of the island, Neloaig (Nelawihang), proclaimed himself John Frum, King of America and of Tanna. He organized an armed force which conscripted labour for the construction of an aerodrome which the Americans had told him to build for American Liberator planes bringing goods from John Frum's father. Those who refused to work would be bombed by planes. This pressed labour was resisted by a few natives who were wounded. The District Agent, under the pretence of demanding a ship to evacuate him from the island, radioed for help. He arrested Neloaig when the latter visited him at his office.

The arrest of Neloaig produced demands for his release. The supporters of John Frum, undaunted, went on feverishly building the airstrip, and a band of Neloaig's followers even attempted to liberate their leader from gaol. The police reinforcements, with two U.S. officers, were quickly despatched to the John Frum airstrip. There they found 200 men at work, surrounded by others with guns. After the latter was disarmed, an American officer spoke to the natives, trying to persuade them of their folly. This was backed up by a demonstration of the power of a tommy-gun turned on a John Frum poster pinned to a nearby tree. Many fled in panic; the police then burned down a John Frum hut and took forty-six prisoners. Neloaig received two years, ten others one year, and the rest three months. Later Neloaig escaped from gaol and hid in the bush on Efate for three years before he gave himself up. In April 1948 he was committed to a lunatic asylum. His wife was detained at Vila, but the people of north Tanna still paid homage to her.

Though illiterate, Neloaig had pretended to read and had started his own schools. When the missionaries at Lenakel tried to restart classes in 1943, only fifty children out of a total population of 2,500 attended. Dances and kava-drinking still flourished, and villages were allowed to fall into untidiness. John Frumism still flourished. Pagans, too, provided recruits; pagan leaders had long attempted to play off Government against mission, Neloaig's father among them.

Peter Worsley, *The Trumpet Shall Sound: A Study of 'Cargo' Cults in Melanesia* (London: MacGibbon & Kee, 1957), pp. 153-9

197. A MESSIANIC NAKED CULT IN SANTO, NEW HEBRIDES

Some time about 1944 or 1945 a curious wave of feeling which we shall call the Naked Cult in imitation of the Santo bushmen themselves, passed over the bush communities of central Santo (i.e., Espiritu Santo). They refer to the followers of the Cult as the *malamala* (naked) folk. . . .

Our trek of 1948 has put a very different complexion on the whole movement. We found that the further we penetrated inland in a westerly direction the more we discovered the people to be affected. We passed through quite a number of villages where the people were openly practising the Cult, and had greatly modified their traditional heathen ways. We even met a measure of hostility—which is signficant in trying to analyse the character of the driving force behind the movement.

It is not easy to judge of the approximate numbers of active followers, but I should estimate it at not less than 500. This represents a proportion of about one-third of the heathen population of those parts of Santo which are affected. Although we called at villages with more than 100 of these followers in them (all told) we did not really penetrate far enough into the western highlands to get to the hearts of the movement. What follows here is, however, the testimony of native chiefs who were intimidated into brief participation in the Cult, or who managed to resist its emissaries when they visited their villages. . . .

Last year all that I could get, in reply to enquiries, was the fact that a man called Tieka (English—Jack) was the moving influence behind the Cult. When I asked where he lived I was vaguely told 'on top'; which is pidgin for 'further inland.' This year I got more information about him. He lives on the Bierai river on the eastern slopes of Tava Masana and has two villages about six miles apart, called Naku and Lori. He is a young man, whom I judge, from inquiry, to be between thirty-five and forty. He has not, so far as my informants knew, ever worked for whites but some of his people have done so, in the past. He is married to two wives (but one informant says only one).

The war was already well towards its close when he started the Cult by sending about thirty of his men—from villages near to his own —on a crusade through the villages of inland Santo. Their message everywhere they went was the same:

1. Take off your loin-cloths. Women take off their leaf coverings. Take off your bead necklaces and armlets. All these things make **you** dirty.

2. Destroy all your property which you have taken from the white man—calico, money, implements; in addition destroy all your own bush crafts such as basket-making and mat-making. It is best to be free from these.

3. Burn down all your present houses and build on the following new plan:

(i) Two big community houses to be erected in each village—one for the men to sleep in at night; and another for the women to sleep in at night. No cohabitation of families at night.

(ii) Build a large kitchen with each community house. No cooking is to be done in the community houses.

4. All food is to be cooked in the *morning*. No night cooking.

5. Do not work for the white man.

6. Destroy all animals in your villages: dogs, cats, pigs, etc.

7. It also appears that they were promised that soon 'America' would come; they would receive everything good; they would never die; they would live for ever.

8. A common language, called 'Maman,' was adopted among all Cult followers even though the villages represent widely separated language groups.

9. Many old taboos have been scrapped; the prohibition on marriage within the totem-group; the segregation period after childbirth; the necessity for buying brides; the burial custom has been changed so that now the corpse is exposed on a wooden platform in the bush (as on parts of Malekula) instead of being buried in the floor of the deceased person's house (as is the tradition in central Santo).

Not every village fell for this. The basic thing was the taking-off of the loin-cloth. In three different villages we were given an interesting account of what actually ensued when the intimidation partly arrived. They were strong enough to overawe the average bush community of twenty to forty souls, and the fact that they repeated their visits showed some determination to force their viewpoint.

J. Graham Miller, 'Naked Cult in Central West Santo,' *The Journal of the Polynesian Society*, vol. 57, (1948), pp. 330-41; quotation from pp. 330-2

Acknowledgments

Bibliography

Index

ACKNOWLEDGMENTS

Acknowledgment is made to the following for permission to reprint copyrighted material:

GEORGE ALLEN AND UNWIN, LTD for extracts from *The Koran,* translated by A. J. Arberry; and *The Teachings of the Magi* by R. C. Zaehner.

BERNICE P. BISHOP MUSEUM for extracts from *Polynesian Religion* by E. S. Craighill Handy, Honolulu: Bernice P. Bishop Museum (Bulletin 34), 1927, quoted with permission.

CAMBRIDGE UNIVERSITY PRESS for extracts from *The Presocratic Philosophers,* translated by G. S. Kirk and J. E. Raven.

BRUNO CASSIRER (PUBLISHERS) LTD for extracts from *Buddhist Texts Through the Ages* edited by Edward Conze (1954).

COLUMBIA UNIVERSITY PRESS for extracts from *Ancient Egyptian Religion* by Henri Frankfort (1948); *Sources of Japanese Tradition,* edited by William Theodore de Bary, copyright © 1958 by Columbia University Press, New York.

COOPER SQUARE PUBLISHERS, INC for extracts from *North American Mythology* by H. B. Alexander.

R. E. DOWNS for extract from *The Religion of the Bare'e-Speaking Toradja of Central Celebes,* published by Uitgeverij Excelsior, 'S-Gravenhage, Netherlands.

THE ESTATE OF WALTER Y. EVANS-WENTZ, DECEASED for extracts from *The Tibetan Book of the Dead* (third edition).

HARVARD UNIVERSITY PRESS for extracts from *Nichiren: the Buddhist Prophet,* reprinted by permission of the publishers.

HARVARD UNIVERSITY PRESS and THE LOEB CLASSICAL LIBRARY for extracts from Homer, *The Odyssey,* vol. II, translated by A. T. Murray; Plato, *Republic,* translated by Paul Shorey; all are reprinted by permission of the publishers and The Loeb Classical Library.

LIBERAL ARTS DIVISION OF THE BOBBS-MERRILL COMPANY INC for extracts from *Ancient Roman Religion,* Frederick C. Grant, editor, copyright © 1957 by the Liberal Arts Press; *Islam: Muhammad and his Religion,* edited by Arthur Jeffery, copyright © 1958 by the Liberal Arts Press.

MACGIBBON AND KEE, LONDON for extracts from *The Trumpet Shall Sound* by Peter Worsley, Macgibbon and Kee, London (1957).

THE MACMILLAN COMPANY for extracts from *The Koran,* translated by A. J. Arberry; *The Teachings of the Magi* by R. C. Zaehner.

METHUEN AND COMPANY LTD for extracts from *Orpheus and the Greek Religion* by W. C. K. Guthrie.

PENGUIN BOOKS LTD, BALTIMORE, MARYLAND for extracts from *Buddhist Scriptures,* edited by Edward Conze.

PENGUIN BOOKS LTD, MIDDLESEX, ENGLAND for extract from *Plato: Protagoras and Meno,* translated by W. C. K. Guthrie.

THE POLYNESIAN SOCIETY (INC), WELLINGTON, NEW ZEALAND for extracts

Acknowledgments

from 'Naked Cult in Central West Santo' by Graham Miller, *Journal of the Polynesian Society,* vol. LVII, (1948).

PRINCETON UNIVERSITY PRESS for extracts from *Ancient Near Eastern Texts Relating to the Old Testament,* edited by James B. Pritchard, reprinted by permission of the Princeton University Press, Copyright 1950.

THAMES AND HUDSON LTD for extracts from *Myth and Symbol in Ancient Egypt* by R. T. Rundle Clark.

UNIVERSITY OF CALIFORNIA PRESS for extracts from *Indian Myths of South Central California* by A. L. Kroeber (University of California Publications in American Archaeology, vol. IV, no. 4, 1906-1907).

THE UNIVERSITY OF CHICAGO PRESS for extracts from *The Iliad,* translated by Richard Lattimore.

THE UNIVERSITY OF NEBRASKA PRESS for extracts reprinted from *The World's Rim* by Hartley Burr Alexander by permission of University of Nebraska Press, copyright 1953, University of Nebraska Press, Lincoln, Nebraska.

BIBLIOGRAPHY

General

On death and disposal of the dead, cf. the bibliographies compiled by J. Wach, *Sociology of Religion* (Chicago, 1944), pp. 66 *ff*. (*nn*. 73-88) and by Friedrich Heiler, *Erscheinungsformen und Wesen der Religion* (Stuttgart, 1961), pp. 515-17. Cf. also E. Brendann, *Death Customs* (London, 1930); B. Y. Jouin, *La mort et la tombe* (Paris, 1949); J. N. Schofield, *Archaeology and the After-life* (London, 1951); G. Pfannmüller, *Tod, Jenseits und Unsterblichkeit* (München-Basel, 1953).

On the primitive conception and beliefs related to death and afterlife, cf. Felix Shercke, *Über das Verhalten der Primitiven zum Tode* (Langensalza, 1923); J. G. Frazer, *The Belief in Immortality and the Worship of the Dead* (3 vols.; London, 1913-24); J. G. Frazer, *The Fear of the Dead in Primitive Religion* (3 vols.; London, 1933-6); Rosalind Moss, *The Life after Death in Oceania and the Malay Archipelago* (London, 1925); Theo. Körner, *Totenkult u. Lebensglauben bei den Völkern Ost-Indonesiens* (Leipzig, 1936); H. J. Sell, *Der schlimme Tod bei den Völkern Indonesiens* (The Hague, 1955); Olof Pettersson, *Jabmek and Jabmeaino: A Comparative Study of the Dead and the Realm of the Dead in Lappish Religion* (Lund, 1957).

Nos. 158-9. On the myth of the descent of Ishtar and the Babylonian conception of death and afterlife, see Alexander Heidel, *The Gilgamesh Epic and Old Testament Parallels* (Chicago, 1946), pp. 119 *ff*.; Erich Ebeling, *Tod und Leben nach den Vorstellungen der Babylonier* (Berlin-Leipzig, 1931).

Nos. 160 *ff*. On the Indo-Aryan conceptions of death, see E. Arbmann, 'Tod und Unsterblichkeit in vedischen Glauben,' *Archiv für Religionswissenschaft*, XXV-XXVI (1927-28), pp. 339-87, 187-240; A. B. Keith, *Religion and Philosophy of the Veda*, Harvard Oriental Series, XXXI-XXXII (Cambridge, Mass., 1925), pp. 413-32; cf. also Kurt Ranke, *Indogermanische Totenverehrung*, I, FF Communications, no. 140 (Helsinki, 1951); Hans Hartmann, *Der Totenkult in Irland* (Heidelberg, 1952).

No. 165. On the Oceanian beliefs, see the works of J. G. Frazer and Rosalind Moss, cited at the beginning of this section, under 'General.'

Nos. 166 *ff*. On the Egyptian funerary ritual and conceptions of the afterlife, see Hans Bonnet, *Reallexikon der ägyptischen Religionsgeschichte* (Berlin, 1952), pp. 828 *ff*.; C. E. Sander-Hansen, *Der Begriff des Todes bei den Ägyptern* (Copenhagen, 1942); J. Zande, *Death as an Enemy, according to Ancient Egyptian Conceptions* (Leiden, 1960).

No. 171. On the gold plates, cf. Jane Harrison, *Prolegomena to the Study of Greek Religion* (Cambridge, England, 1903), pp. 583 *ff*.; W. K. C. Guthrie, *Orpheus and the Greek Religion* (London, 1935), pp. 171 *ff*.

No. 172. On the Iranian conceptions of a future life, cf. N. Söderblom, *La vie future d'après le Mazdéisme* (Paris, 1901); J. D. C. Pavry, *The Zoroastrian*

Bibliography

Doctrine of a Future Life (2nd ed.; New York, 1929).

On the judgment of the dead in the Ancient Near East, India, China, Japan, etc., see *Le jugement des morts* ('Sources Orientales,' vol. IV [Paris, 1961]).

No. 173. On the shaman as the guide of the soul, see M. Eliade, *Shamanism: Archaic Techniques of Ecstasy* (New York and London, 1964).

Nos. 178 ff. On the Greek and Roman conceptions of death and afterlife, see Erwin Rohde, *Psyche: The Cult of Souls and Belief in Immortality among the Greeks* (New York and London, 1925); Franz Cumont, *After-Life in Roman Paganism* (New Haven, 1923); F. Cumont, *Lux perpetua* (Paris, 1949); C. H. Moore, *Ancient Beliefs in the Immortality of the Soul: Our Debt to Greece and Rome* (New York, 1931).

On the Oriental and early Christian representations of the nether world, see André Parrot, *Le 'Refrigerium' dans l'au-delà* (Paris, 1937).

Nos. 184-5. On the Polynesian 'Orpheus' myths, see M. Eliade, *Shamanism, op. cit.,* pp. 368 ff. On the North American 'Orpheus' myths, see *ibid.,* pp. 311 ff., and Åke Hultkrantz, *The North American Indian Orpheus Tradition* (Stockholm, 1957).

No. 186. On messianic ideologies in India, see E. Abegg, *Der Messiasglaube in Indien und Iran* (Berlin, 1928).

No. 187. On the Islamic conceptions of Paradise, see Miguel Asin Palacios, *La escatologia musulmana en la Divina Comedia* (2nd ed.; Madrid-Granada, 1943).

Nos. 188 ff. On the myths describing the end of the world, see W. Bousset, *The Antichrist Legend* (London, 1896); Alex Olrik, *Ragnorök, die Sagen vom Weltuntergang* (Berlin, 1922); Jan de Vries, *Altgermanische Religionsgeschichte,* vol. II (2nd ed.; Berlin, 1957), pp. 392-405; M. Eliade, *Myth and Reality* (New York, 1963), pp. 54ff., chap. IV, 'Eschatology and Cosmogony'.

No. 189. E. Lamotte, 'Prophéties relatives à la disparition de la Bonne Loi,' in René de Berval (ed.), *Présence du Bouddhisme* (Saigon, 1959), pp. 657-68.

No. 190. On Zoroastrian ideas concerning the end of the world, see R. C. Zaehner, *The Dawn and Twilight of Zoroastrianism* (London, 1961), pp. 312 ff.

Nos. 191 ff. On the Islamic beliefs, see Regnar Eklund, *Life between Death and Resurrection according to Islam* (Uppsala, 1941).

Nos. 194 ff. On cargo cults and modern messianic movements, cf. P. Worsley, *The Trumpet Shall Sound* (London, 1957); K. O. L. Burridge, *Mambu: A Melanesian Millennium* (London, 1960); G. Guariglia, *Prophetismus und Heilserwartungsbewegungen als völkerkundliches und religionsgeschichtliches Problem* (Horn-Wien, 1953); Sylvia L. Thrupp (ed.), *Millennial Dreams in Action: Essays in Comparative Study* (The Hague, 1962); Vittorio Lanternari, *The Religions of the Oppressed: A Study of Modern Messianic Cults* (New York and London, 1963); Wilhelm E. Mühlmann, *Chiliasmus und Nativismus* (Berlin, 1961); I. C. Jarvie, 'Theories of Cargo Cults: A Critical Analysis,' *Oceania,* XXXIV (1963), pp. 1-31, 108-36; M. Eliade, *Mephistopheles and the Androgyne* (New York, 1966, British ed. *The Two and the One,* London, 1965), pp. 125-59; 'Cosmic and Eschatological Renewal.'

Nos. 194-5. For a bibliography of some major writings on the Ghost Dance published after 1896, see Anthony F. C. Wallace, Introduction to the new edition of James Mooney's *Ghost-Dance Religion and the Sioux Outbreak of 1890* (Chicago, 1965), pp. VIII ff.

ETHNIC AND GEOGRAPHIC
CROSS-REFERENCE INDEX